Card Games
for One

Card Games
for One

Peter Arnold

hamlyn

First published in Great Britain in 2002 by Hamlyn,
a division of Octopus Publishing Group Ltd
2–4 Heron Quays, London E14 4JP

Copyright © Octopus Publishing Group Ltd 2002

Distributed in the United States and Canada by
Sterling Publishing Co., Inc.
387 Park Avenue South,
New York, NY 10016–8810

ISBN 0 600 60727 5

A CIP catalogue record for this book is available from the
British Library

Page make-up and illustrations by
Publish on Demand Ltd.

Card designs based on Waddingtons No. 1 Playing Cards.

WADDINGTONS NO. 1 PLAYING CARDS ©
2002 Hasbro Inc.
Used with kind permission.

Printed and bound in United Arab Emirates

10 9 8 7 6 5 4 3 2 1

Contents

Introduction

The origins of patience games, or solitaire as they are called in the United States, are unknown. The first written references to them come much later than references to card games for two or more. But as the first use of playing cards (the tarot pack) was for divination it would be strange to think that nobody was inspired by elaborate fortune-telling layouts to invent a way of adapting them for solitary amusement.

The earliest references to patience appear in France and Germany towards the end of the 18th century. The first book of patience games published in England dates from about 1870 (only a second edition exists, dated 1874). It was entitled *Illustrated Games of Patience* and was written by Lady Adelaide Cadogan. She described 24 games, many with French names, suggesting sources in France. One such, Le Cadran, is included in this book. Charles Dickens referred to patience before this, however, in *Pickwick Papers*, published in 1861, and it is known that Prince Albert, consort of Queen Victoria, who died in that year, played patience.

Tolstoy referred to a game of patience in *War and Peace*, written in the 1860s, although that game was supposed to have taken place in 1808. Dostoevsky also referred to patience in *The Brothers Karamazov*, written in the 1880s. The most famous person alleged to have a weakness for patience is Napoleon, who supposedly passed hours of exile on St Helena playing various games before his death in 1821. Many patience games commemorate Napoleon, but it is unlikely that he ever played them. St Helena, included in this book, is also known as Napoleon's Favourite (and sometimes Washington's Favourite).

Hundreds of patience games were invented in the 20th century. This book includes a selection of the best. Apart from a few, which I have written specially for this book, the descriptions have been taken, slightly edited, from earlier books published by Hamlyn, and were written by the late Mr George F. Hervey, Matthew Macfadyen and myself. Of these, the majority were written by Mr Hervey, a witty and excellent writer on card games, and it is a pleasure for me to see his work still widely in circulation.

The current book contains patiences composed by Mr Charles Jewell, acknowledged in the text. Mr Hervey invented one game himself, Crossword, which first appeared with his modest aside: 'An ill-favoured thing, sir, but mine own.' The present writer has included a cribbage patience invented by himself, and might, with a deferent nod to the shade of Mr Hervey, claim that it is 'an even more ill-favoured thing, sir, than yours'.

Peter Arnold, 2002

Accordion

HOW TO PLAY

There is no starting layout and the cards are shuffled and dealt from the hand one at a time. The first card is dealt to the top left of the board and succeeding cards to the right of the one before, so a row is built up from left to right. The object is to finish with all the cards in one pack.

If when it is dealt a card matches its left-hand neighbour either in suit or rank it can be packed on it. Similarly, if it matches the card three places to its left (i.e. with two other cards intervening) it can be packed upon that. If a card can be packed in either position, the player chooses which option to take. When a card topping a pile is moved, the whole pile moves with it. All moves should be carried out as soon as they become possible.

If a long string of cards is built up, it is often easier to start a second or third row, in which case the lines are to be considered continuous. Often the length of the line expands and contracts, like the musical instrument after which the game is named. Success is almost entirely a matter of chance, and is rarely achieved. To finish with no more than three piles is a good result.

In the illustration, if the next card dealt is the ♣6, it can be packed on the ♠6, the pile topped by the ♣Q packed on it, the ♥3 packed on the ♥8 and the ♣Q pile packed on the ♣10, thus reducing the piles to two. If the next card dealt were the ♣3 or ♥Q, they would be reduced to one. Notice that the ♥3 must be packed on the ♥8 before the ♣Q is packed on the ♣10 – otherwise it will not go.

Card dealt

Agnes

HOW TO PLAY

Deal to the board 28 cards face up in one row of seven cards, one of six, and so on, down to one card. For convenience the rows may overlap. The twenty-ninth card is dealt face up to the centre as a foundation card. As they become available, either from the layout or the hand, the other three cards of the same rank will be placed in line with it (see illustration).

The object of the game is to build ascending, round-the-corner suit sequences onto the foundation cards.

The bottom card of a column in the layout is termed exposed. It may be built on a foundation or packed on another exposed card in the layout. Within the layout, cards are packed in descending sequences of the same colour (not necessarily of the same suit), but it should be borne in mind that a sequence may be moved from one column to another only as a whole and only if all the cards of the sequence are of the same suit. If a vacancy occurs through all the cards of a column being moved, it may be filled with any available card, or same-suit sequence of cards, if wished.

After all possible moves have been made, cards are dealt face up to the bottom of all the columns, and the game continues until the stock is exhausted.

After the third deal has been made from the stock, there will be two cards

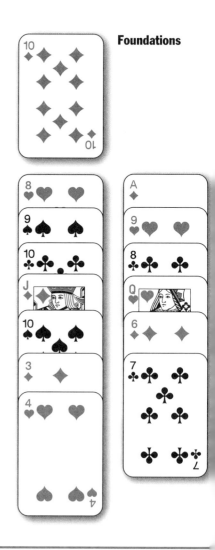

Foundations

left in the hand and these may be played to either a foundation or the layout.

In the illustration, play the ♥10 to the foundation row. Pack the ♥5 on the ♥6 and the ♥4 on the ♥5. Pack the ♠2 on the ♣3, and the ♠6 on the ♣7. Move the ♦Q into the vacancy, and pack the ♥6,

♥5 and ♥4 together on the ♥7. Pack the ♣5 on the ♠6 and move the ♥7, ♥6, ♥5 and ♥4 together into the vacancy. Then deal seven more cards and continue.

Baker's dozen

It is reported that in ancient Egypt, a baker selling loaves of insufficient weight faced the possiblity of being nailed to the door of his shop by the ear. In 1266, when the English parliament passed a law exacting penalties on bakers who baked underweight loaves, the bakers decided to add a thirteenth loaf to each dozen delivered to retailers, thus guarding against a loaf being light. A 'baker's dozen' thus came to be thirteen. This game perhaps gets its name from the number of rows in the layout.

HOW TO PLAY

Deal the complete pack face up in 13 piles of four cards each. Move the Kings to the bottom of their piles, and spread the piles out so that all four cards may be seen (see illustration).

The object of the game is to play the Aces, as they become available, to the centre as foundations and to build ascending suit sequences to the Kings on them.

Only the top card of a pile may be lifted and built on a foundation, or packed in descending sequence, regardless of suit and colour, on the top card of another pile. When all the cards of a pile have been moved, the vacancy is not filled.

In the illustration, the ♥3 is packed on the ♣4, the ♠A is played to the centre and the ♠2 and ♠3 built on it. The ♠6 is packed on the ♠7, the ♣A is played to the centre and the ♣2 built on it. The ♠4 is packed on the ♣5, the ♦A is played to the centre and the ♦2 and ♦3 built on it, and so on until no more moves may be made.

Watch out for two cards of the same suit being in the same column of the layout, with the higher card being available for play first (such as the ♥A and ♥2 in the first column illustrated and the ♦4 and ♦J in the third column). Clearly the ♥2 or the ♦J cannot be played to a foundation without being played to another place in the layout first, thus releasing the ♥A and ♦4. You must therefore try to play these cards as early as you can.

Beleaguered castle

Beleaguered Castle, also called Laying Siege and Sham Battle, has a pleasing tableau although it must be admitted that it can be a frustrating game.

HOW TO PLAY

The four Aces are removed from the pack and placed in a column in the centre of the table to form the foundations. The remainder of the pack is shuffled and a column of four cards is dealt to the left of the Aces, followed by a column to the right of the Aces. Succeeding columns are dealt alternately on these, with each column overlapping the last until the whole pack is dealt and the tableau resembles the illustration. The cards to the left of the Aces are called the left wing and those to the right the right wing.

The object is to build suit sequences up to the Kings on the foundations. Only the cards at the far end of each row, i.e. those whose faces are fully exposed, are available for play. They can be built directly onto the foundations or packed onto another available card in descending order of rank, irrespective of suit, e.g. a 6 can be packed on any 7. When one of the rows is emptied, it can be filled by any available card. There are thus always eight available cards for play.

In the illustration, the ♥2 and ♠2 can be played to the foundations; the ♦4 to ♦5; ♣5 to ♦6; ♦3 to ♦4; ♦2 to foundation; ♦3, 4, 5 to foundation; ♠6 to ♦7; ♣4 to ♣5; ♣Q to ♣K; ♥6 to ♥7; ♦K to the space created in the rows; ♥9 to ♦10; ♠5 to ♠6; ♣3 to ♣4; ♣2 to foundation, thus clearing another row and allowing the club foundation to be built on. But the game is soon doomed to failure, there being too many high cards burying the lower ones. The game is a quick one and the player will soon be optimistically redealing, which is the usual way with patience games.

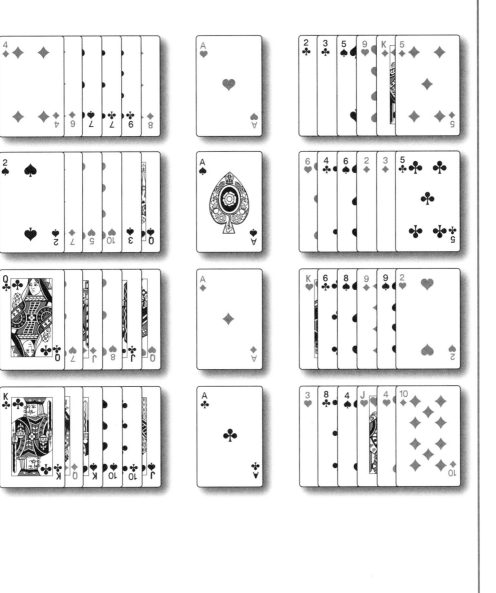

Belvedere

HOW TO PLAY

Remove any Ace from the pack and play it to the centre as the first foundation card. Deal 24 cards face up to the board in eight fans of three cards each (any King dealt should be moved to the bottom of its fan) and then three cards in a row, below layout, as a reserve (see illustration).

The object of the game is to release the other three Aces, play them to the centre as foundation cards, and build ascending sequences on the four Aces, regardless of suit and colour, to the Kings.

The top cards of the fans and the top cards in the reserve are exposed and may be built on the foundation. In the layout, the top cards of the fans may be packed on each other in descending sequences regardless of suit and colour. The top cards of the reserve may also be packed on a fan, but cards in the reserve are not packed upon. Only one card may be moved at a time.

A vacancy in the layout, when all the cards of a fan have been played, is not filled.

The stock is dealt three cards at a time, one card to cover each card of the reserve and to fill any vacancies in it. The game ends when all the cards in the stock have been dealt.

In the illustration, the ♦J is packed on the ♣Q, the ♦7 on the ♦8, the ♦6 on the ♦7 and the ♦5 on the ♦6. The ♠A is played to the foundation row and the ♠2 built on it. The ♥7 is packed on the ♠8, the ♦J on the ♠Q, the ♣Q on the ♠K, the ♦J on the ♣Q, the ♠10 on the ♦J and the ♥9 on the ♠10. The ♥A is then played to the foundation row and further cards may be packed or built onto the foundations as they are released.

Foundation

Layout

Reserve

Bisley

HOW TO PLAY

Place the Aces face up in a row on the table. Deal nine cards in a row to the right of them, and the rest of the pack in three rows of 13 cards below them (see illustration). As the four Kings become available, place them above their respective Aces.

The player builds up on the Aces and down on the Kings in same-suit sequences. It does not matter where the two sequences meet.

Only the bottom card in a column is available for play. It may be built onto either its Ace or King foundation, packed on the bottom card of another column, or have another card packed onto it.

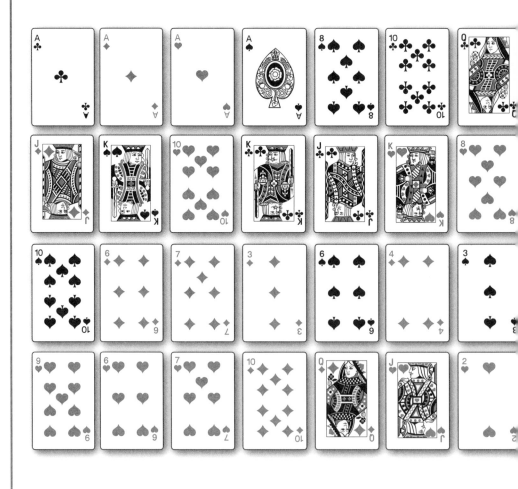

Packing may be either up or down in suit sequence. A space left vacant in the layout by the removal of the last card in a column is not filled.

In the layout illustrated, the ♦ K is played above the ♦ A, the ♠ 2 is built on the ♠ A, and the ♥ 2 on the ♥ A. This exposes the ♠ 3, which is built on the ♠ 2. The ♦ Q is built on the ♦ K. The ♦ 9 is packed on the ♦ 10, and the ♦ 8 on the ♦ 9. Now the ♣ 8 is packed on the ♣ 9, exposing the ♣ 2, which is built on the ♣ A. Further cards are then played until the game is won or no more moves can be played.

Block eleven

*Block Eleven, or Calling Out, will occupy a couple of minutes if you are so
unlucky as to have a couple of minutes with nothing better to occupy them.*

HOW TO PLAY

Remove the first 12 numeral cards (i.e.
Ace to 10) from the pack and play them
face up to the board in three rows of four,
or four rows of three: it doesn't matter
which. Shuffle the rest of the cards until
a picture card lies at the bottom of the
pack – if you do not, the game cannot
be won.

Where, added together, two cards in
the layout total 11, a card is dealt on each
from the stock. Once a picture card has

been dealt on one of the piles, no more
cards can be added to it. The game is
won when all 40 cards of the stock have
been dealt and the 12 picture cards cover
the layout. It is an inane game that
requires no skill, but does have a pretty
ending.

In the illustration of a game in
progress, four piles have so far been
blocked by picture cards. Play continues
by placing cards from the stock on one
of the 8s and the ♦3, and on the ♠9
and ♦2.

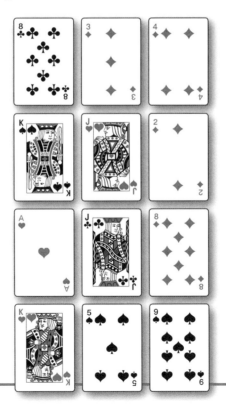

Calculation

Calculation, or Broken Intervals, is well named, because it is necessary to calculate at the turn of every card and it offers great scope for skilful play.

HOW TO PLAY

Any Ace, any 2, any 3 and any 4 are placed in a row on the table to form four foundations. The object of the game is to build, regardless of suits, the remaining 48 cards on them, in the following order:

On the Ace – 2, 3, 4, 5, 6, 7, 8, 9, 10, Jack, Queen, King
On the 2 – 4, 6, 8, 10, Queen, Ace, 3, 5, 7, 9, Jack, King
On the 3 – 6, 9, Queen, 2, 5, 8, Jack, Ace, 4, 7, 10, King
On the 4 – 8, Queen, 3, 7, Jack, 2, 6, 10, Ace, 5, 9, King

The cards are dealt from the pack one at a time and every card must either be built on a foundation or played to any of the four waste heaps below the foundation (see illustration). At any time the top card of a waste heap may be built on a foundation, but it may not be played to another waste heap. The pack is dealt only once, but play from a waste heap may continue after it is exhausted.

The cards in the pack are now dealt one at a time. Suppose a 10 is dealt, as it cannot be built on a foundation it is best played to a vacant waste heap. Next a 6 is dealt; it is built on the 3 foundation. Next comes an 8, and is built on the 4 foundation. The next card is a King. It must be played to a waste heap, but because the Kings are the last cards to be built on the foundations it would be wrong to play it to, for example, the waste heap containing the 10. It should be played to another waste heap, and experienced players would now reserve this for Kings. Play continues in this way until all 48 cards have been dealt.

If the play is carefully thought out, by building cards on the waste heaps in descending sequences of two to four or, hopefully, more, excellent progress will be made towards the end of the game.

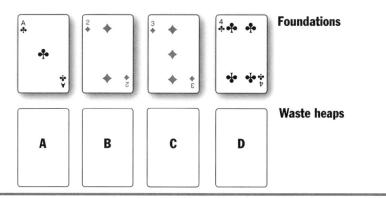

Foundations

Waste heaps

Captive queens

Captive Queens is a variation of another game called Quadrille. As is common with patience games, the two are often confused.

HOW TO PLAY

Remove the four Queens and set them into the pattern shown in illustration 1 (below). They take no part in the game – their purpose is decorative. Cards are turned up from the stock into a face-up waste pile one at a time. As the 5s and 6s become available they are played to the table in the positions shown in

Illustration 1

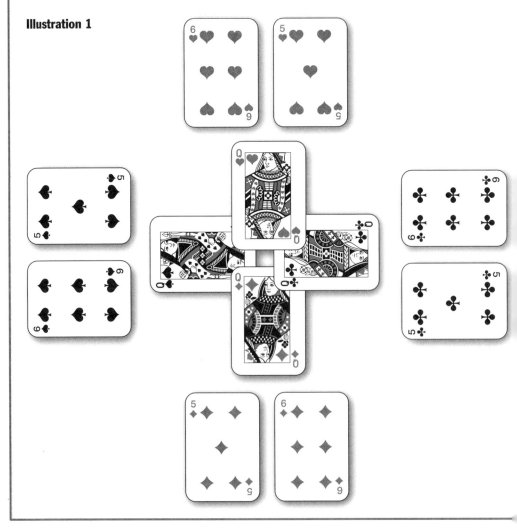

illustration 1. These are the foundation cards and cards are built on them as they become available. The 6s are built in suits up to the Jacks. The 5s are built down in suit to the Kings, i.e. 4, 3, 2, Ace, King. Cards that cannot be played to a foundation are put into a face-up waste pile, the top card of which is always available for play.

When the stock is exhausted, the waste pile can be turned over (but not shuffled) and redealt twice. A successful game ends with each Queen under the watchful eye of her King and Jack (see illustration 2, below).

Illustration 2

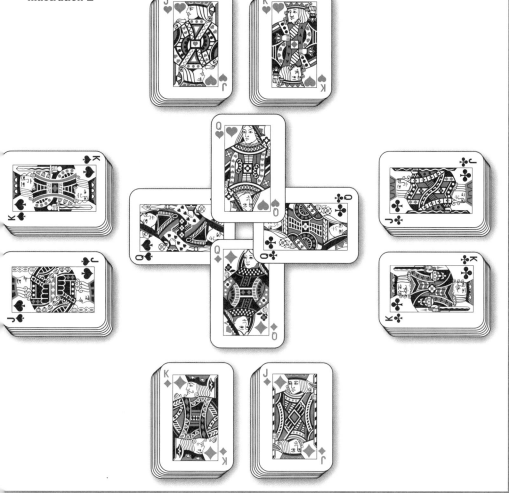

The carpet

HOW TO PLAY

Remove the four Aces from the pack and play them to the centre as foundations. Below them deal 20 cards face up in four rows of five cards each (see illustration).

The object of the game is to build ascending suit sequences to the Kings on the Aces.

All of the cards in the layout (the carpet) may be built on the foundations, and the resulting vacancies are filled from the waste heap or from the stock if there is no waste heap.

Cards cannot be packed on the layout. The stock is turned one card at a time and any card that cannot be built on a foundation is played to the waste heap, the top card of which is always available to be played.

In the illustration the ♣2 is built on the ♣A, the ♣3 on the ♣2 and the ♣4 on the ♣3. The ♦2 is built on the ♦A and the ♦3 on the ♦2. The five vacancies are filled from the stock and play continues.

The game ends when the stock has been dealt once.

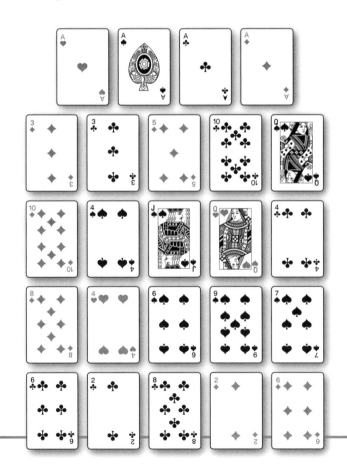

Clock

This is a simple five-minute game that relies entirely on chance.

HOW TO PLAY

First, 13 piles of four cards are dealt face down one at a time, 12 in a circle to represent the numbers on a clock face and the thirteenth in the centre. The top card of the centre pile is turned over and placed behind the pile representing its number on the clock face (Jacks count as 11 and Queens 12). The top card of that pile is then exposed and placed in its appropriate position, and a card from that pile exposed. When a King is exposed it is played to the centre and another card exposed from there. The object is to end with all cards exposed.

Once the fourth King is exposed, the game ends, as there is not another card in the centre to turn over. For the game to succeed, therefore, the last card exposed must be a King, so the chance of success is one in 13.

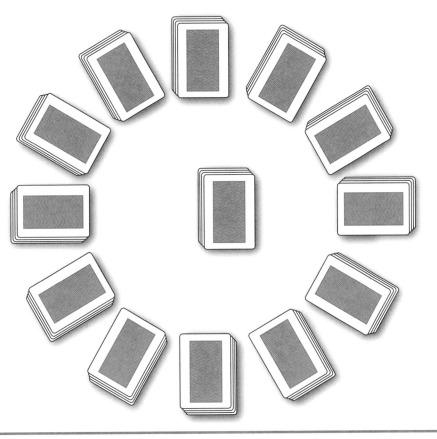

Cribbage patience

There are many forms of patience invented to satisfy addicts of cribbage who are missing an opponent. This is one of the simplest and a game can be played in five minutes.

HOW TO PLAY

From a shuffled pack, deal two hands of six cards each. Set the remainder of the pack aside as the stock. Pick up the first hand. Arrange it into a four-card cribbage hand, laying away the other two cards face up to start a crib. Examine the second hand and contribute two more cards to the crib. Turn over the top card of the stock as the start. The two hands and the crib are then scored as they would be in the show at cribbage.

The start is combined with each hand in turn, making each in effect consist of five cards. With court cards counting as ten, points are scored as follows:

Fifteens: Each combination of two or more cards held that total 15 (for example Jack, 5; 8, 7) scores two points.
Pairs: Each pair scores two points.
Runs: For each run, irrespective of suit, of three or more, the number of cards in the run is scored.

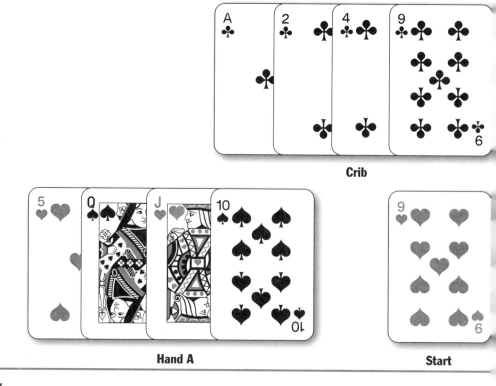

Crib

Hand A

Start

Flush: For four cards of the same suit held in either of the hands, four points are scored. If the start is also of the same suit, five points are scored. A flush is only scored in the crib, however, if the start is of the same suit, in which case five points are scored.

His nob and his heels: The jack of the same suit as the start scores one point 'for his nob'; if the start is a jack, two points are scored 'for his heels'.

Once the score has been taken for all three hands, the hands and the start (totalling 13 cards) are discarded, and another hand dealt. Four deals, which use all 52 cards, constitute a game. For players who like the challenge of a game that very rarely succeeds, a target of 121 points (the usual score needed to win a game of cribbage) is recommended. For those who like a success rate of about one in three, a score of 101 is suggested. Addicts will soon find they spend too much time trying to beat their lifetime record (a best of 130 might indicate an urgent need to discover some other interests).

In the illustration, hand A scores 11 (six for fifteens, four for a run, one for his nob); hand B scores 12 (six for fifteens, six for pairs); the crib scores six (four for fifteens, two for a pair). This makes a total of 29 for the deal, which is an excellent score.

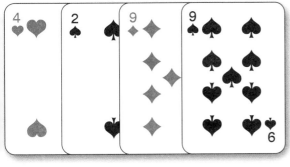

Hand B

Crossword

HOW TO PLAY

The 12 court cards are removed from the pack and temporarily set aside. The top card of the pack is played to the board, and the rest of the pack is turned one card at a time. Each card in turn is played to the board in a position adjoining a card already played, at top or bottom, to either side, or diagonally.

The object of the game is to complete a square – seven cards in each direction – in which the pips of the cards in each row and column add up to an even number. The court cards do not count, but are brought into the game when needed to serve as stops, much the same as the black squares in a crossword puzzle; at least nine, and probably all of them, will have to be used. Bear in mind that the pips of the cards between two court cards, or between a court card and the outer edge of the square, must also add up to an even number (see illustration).

When there is only one square to fill, the player may look at the four cards in the hand and choose one needed to complete the game.

Demon

Demon is probably the best known of all one-pack patiences. It is sometimes known as Fascination, sometimes as Thirteen, and, in the USA, as Canfield, because it was reputedly invented by Richard A. Canfield, a well-known, late 19th-century gambler, who used to sell the pack for $52 and pay $5 for every card in the foundation row when the game came to an end. It was not altogether as profitable as it might seem, because he had to employ one croupier to keep an eye on each player during the play.

HOW TO PLAY

Deal 13 cards face down in a pile and turn the top card face up. This pile is known as the heel. Then deal four cards face up in a row to the right of the heel and place a fifth face up and above the first card of the row (see illustration). This is the first of four foundations. The object of the game is to build round-the-corner sequences on the foundations.

In the illustration, the ♦10 is the first foundation, and the ♦3 is the top card of the heel. As they become available, the other three 10s will be played to the right of the ♦10. The four cards to the right of the heel are packed in descending sequences of alternating colours. As a start, therefore, the ♦J is built on its foundation card; the ♣4 is packed on the ♥5 and the ♦3 on the ♣4. The card in the heel below the ♦3 is turned and, if it cannot be built on a foundation or packed on a card in the layout, is played to the space left vacant by the ♦J. The next card in the heel is then exposed.

The bottom card in any of the four columns may be built onto a foundation.

However, a sequence may be packed on the next higher card in sequence in another column only as a whole.

The stock is dealt to a waste pile in batches of three cards at a time, but if there are fewer than three cards at the end of the stock they are dealt singly. The stock is dealt and redealt until the game is won, or lost because no further move can be made.

When all the cards in a column have been played, the space that is left must be filled at once with the top card of the heel and the next card of the heel exposed. When the heel is exhausted, spaces are filled from the waste heap, and the player need no longer fill a space at once, but can leave it vacant until a suitable card is available. Spaces are never filled from the cards in the hand.

Eagle wings

Eagle Wings, or 13 Down, is one of those games that depends for success entirely on the order in which the cards are dealt.

HOW TO PLAY

Deal 13 cards to the board face down in a pile (the heel). On each side of the heel four cards are dealt face up in a row (the wings). Above the heel a card is dealt face up as the first foundation (see illustration). As they become available the other three cards of the same rank will be placed in the row with it.

The object of the game is to build same-suit, round-the-corner sequences on the foundation cards. The eight cards in the wings are available to be played to the foundations, and the vacancies are filled with cards from the heel turned face up. The stock is dealt one card at a time, and any card that cannot be played to a foundation is played to a waste heap. When only one card remains in the heel it is turned face up and may be played direct to a foundation, without first filling a vacancy in the wings. When the heel is exhausted any vacancy in the wings may be filled with a card from either the stock or the waste heap.

The stock may be dealt three times in all, but must not be shuffled between deals. You won't win.

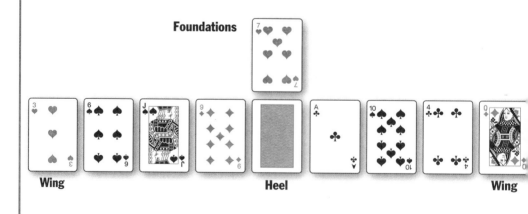

Foundations

Wing   **Heel**   **Wing**

Easy go

HOW TO PLAY

Play the four Aces to the centre as foundation cards. Below them deal 12 cards face up in any convenient arrangement (see illustration).

The object of the game is to build ascending suit sequences to the Kings on the Aces. All of the cards in the layout are exposed and may be built on the foundations. They may also be packed on each other in descending suit sequences, but only one card at a time may be moved from one pile in the layout to another. A vacancy in the layout is filled either from the waste heap or the stock.

The stock is dealt one card at a time and a card that cannot be built on a foundation or packed on the layout is played to a waste heap, the top card of which is always available to be played. The stock is dealt only once.

In the illustration the ♦2 is built on the ♦A. The ♣3 is packed on the ♣4 and the ♦5 on the ♦6. If the ♦7 is dealt from the stock it may be packed on the ♦8, but the ♦6 with the ♦5 cannot be packed on the ♦7. The game continues until no more moves can be made.

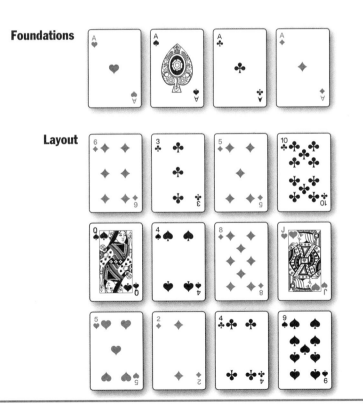

Foundations

Layout

Eight off

A fascinating game for an idle quarter of an hour, with an estimated chance of winning one in two games.

HOW TO PLAY

Deal the pack face up to the board in six overlapping rows of eight cards each, playing the Aces as they occur to a foundation row (see illustration).

The object of the game is to build suit sequences to the Kings on the Aces.

The bottom card of any column is exposed so once it has been played the card immediately above it becomes exposed and available. The game's name derives from the fact that the player may take up to eight (but no more) exposed cards into the hand. These cards are collectively known as the reserve and are retained in hand until they are required for building on a foundation or for packing on an exposed card in a column.

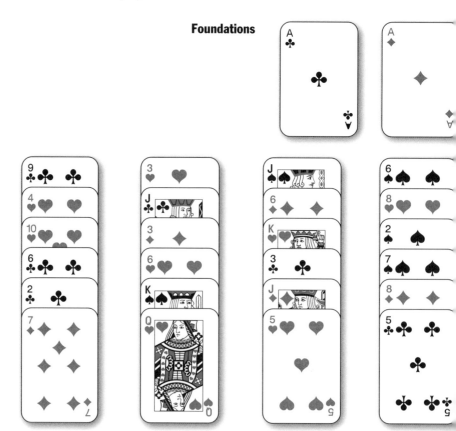

Foundations

Exposed cards at the foot of columns may be built on a foundation, or packed on another exposed card in descending suit sequence. Only one card may be moved at a time.

A vacancy caused by all the cards of a column being played may only be filled by a King.

In the layout illustrated, the ♦Q is packed on the ♦K, the ♠8 on the ♠9 and the ♣5 taken into the reserve. The ♦7 is packed on the ♦8 and the ♣2 built on the ♣A. The ♥5 is taken into the reserve, the ♦J packed on the ♦Q and the ♣3 built on the ♣2. The ♦7 and ♦8 are taken into the reserve, the ♠7 packed on the ♠8 and the ♠2 built on the ♠A.

TACTICS

A player's first aim should be to release low cards and build them on the foundations. Retain as many openings as possible in the reserve – they are more important than creating vacancies in the layout, which may be filled only by a King.

Florentine

HOW TO PLAY

Deal five cards face up to the board in the form of a cross, then deal the sixth card to the centre as the first of the four foundations (see illustration). As the other three cards of the same rank as the foundation card are dealt, they are added to the centre as foundations.

The object of the game is to build ascending, round-the-corner suit sequences on the foundation cards.

The card in the centre of the cross may not be packed on, but the remaining cards in the cross are available for building on the foundations or for packing on each other in descending sequence regardless of suit and colour. When one of these cards is built on a foundation, or packed on another card of the cross, the vacancy is filled either with the top card of the waste heap or with the centre card of the cross and the vacancy in the centre of the cross filled with the top card of the waste heap. Cards are dealt from the stock one at a time and those that cannot be built or packed are played to a waste heap. One redeal is allowed by turning the waste heap, but it may not be shuffled.

In the game in progress in the illustration, the foundation cards are to be built up to their respective 7s. The ♦6 is packed on the ♠7 and the vacancy filled with the ♠10, or with the ♣2 and the ♠10 played to the centre of the cross. And so on.

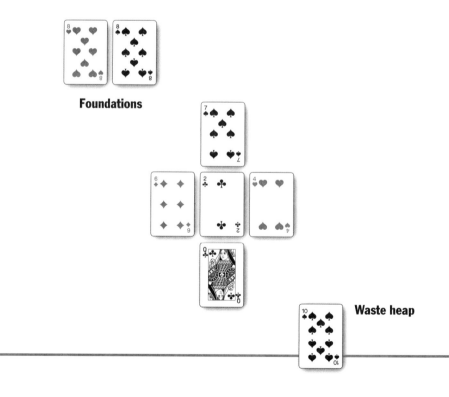

Foundations

Waste heap

Flower garden

The Flower Garden, sometimes called the Bouquet and sometimes the Garden, is a fascinating one-pack patience with the added merit that some degree of skill is needed.

Six packets of six cards each are fanned on the table. They are known as the beds (see illustration overleaf). The remaining 16 cards are retained in the hand and are known collectively as the bouquet.

The object of the game is to release the four Aces, play them to a row above the beds, and build on them ascending suit sequences to the Kings.

While only the right-hand card in a bed is exposed, all of the cards in the bouquet are exposed and may either be built on the Ace foundations or packed on the outer card of a bed in descending sequence irrespective of suit and colour. A sequence may be moved from one bed to another provided the sequence is retained. When a bed has been cleared, the vacant space may be filled either with a card from the bouquet, or by an exposed card or sequence from another bed.

In the layout illustrated, the ♣A is played to the foundation row, the ♣2 built on it, followed by the ♣3 from the bouquet. The ♦Q is packed on the ♦K, and the ♦J on the ♦Q, followed by the ♦10 from the bouquet then the ♥9, ♠8 and the ♠7. Now the ♠6 is packed on the ♠7 and the ♦A played to the foundation row. The ♦5 is packed on the ♠6, the ♣6 on the ♦7 and the ♠2 on the ♠3.

TACTICS

At the best of times this patience is not an easy game and this particular hand will be difficult to win because of the high cards in the bouquet and on top of the beds. Packing a card from the bouquet on a bed should be avoided where an alternative play is possible, because reducing the number of cards in the bouquet reduces the number of cards that may be played at any one time. For the same reason, an empty bed is not always advantageous, and it is unwise to pack too many cards on one bed in order to empty another. The main aim of the player should be to release the Aces, 2s and 3s, because a game may well be lost if even one low card is immobilized, and certainly if two are.

Layout (six fans)

Bouquet

Fortune

HOW TO PLAY

Remove the four Aces from the pack and play them to the centre as foundation cards. Below them deal 12 cards face up. For convenience, these may be arranged on the board in three rows of four cards each (see illustration).

The object of the game is to build ascending suit sequences to the Kings on the Aces.

The cards in the layout are available to be built on the foundations, or packed in descending suit sequences. Only one card may be moved at a time.

The stock is dealt one card at a time and any card that cannot be built on a foundation or packed on the layout is played to a waste heap, the top card of which is always available for play.

Any vacancy in the layout is filled with the top card of the waste heap, or the top card from the stock if there is no waste heap. Only one deal is allowed.

With the layout in the illustration, the ♦2 is built on the ♦A. The ♠5 is packed on the ♠6 and the ♠4 on the ♠5. The ♣8 is packed on the ♣9, and the ♦9 on the ♦10, followed by cards from the waste heap or stock as necessary.

Foundations

Layout

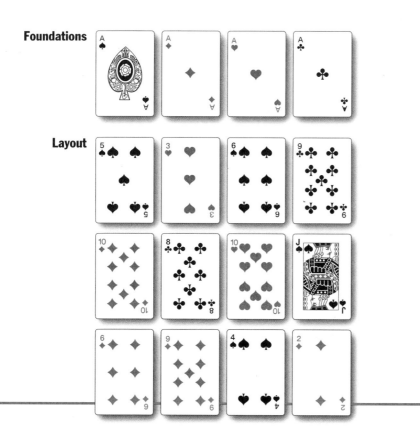

Golf

Golf is a patience game, but addicts of the real game of golf might like to play it against an opponent, as described below.

HOW TO PLAY

Seven cards are dealt face up in a row, and second, third, fourth and fifth rows are dealt, each overlapping the previous row, until 35 cards are dealt in a tableau as shown in the illustration. This tableau is known as the 'links'.

The remainder of the cards are held in the hand and dealt one at a time to a talon or waste heap. Any of the cards exposed in the bottom row of the links is available to play onto the top card of the talon in either ascending or descending order, irrespective of suit. As many cards as possible may be played onto the talon at a turn, and the sequence may go up and down at will. However, the sequence does not go round the corner, so that Aces cannot be played onto Kings or vice versa.

When a card has been removed from the bottom row, the card beneath it becomes available for play.

The object is to clear as many cards from the links as possible by the time the cards in the hand have run out. The number of cards remaining in the links is the score for the hole. To establish a player's score for the round, 18 such holes are played. Sometimes the links will be cleared before all the cards in hand are exhausted, in which case the cards in hand represent a minus score for

the hole, and can be deducted from a player's total. The object when played purely as a patience game is to beat par: 72 'strokes'.

In the layout in the illustration, the ♦7 has been turned over as the first card from hand onto the waste heap. Cards from the links can be played onto the ♦7 as follows: ♠8, ♦9, ♦10, ♥J, ♥Q, ♣J, ♣10. This is quite a good start. Then the next card from the hand is turned over,

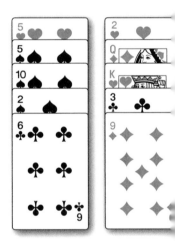

any further possible moves made, and then the rest of the cards in turn.

COMPETITIVE GOLF

Golf patience can be played as a competitive game for two or more players. Each player has his or her own pack and deals 35 cards into a links as above. All of the players play each hole simultaneously and record scores for the 18 holes, the one with the lowest total being the winner.

Two players can play 'match play', in which instead of recording the score for

each hole, each hole is either won, lost or halved, so that at any stage a player is 'two up', 'three down', etc. as in the real game. Four players can play as a 'four ball', i.e. in two partnerships, with each player using his own pack and only the lower score of each pair counting.

It is well known that patience players face a great temptation to cheat from time to time. Of course, players taking part in Competitive Golf must be as scrupulous over the rules as their counterparts out on the course.

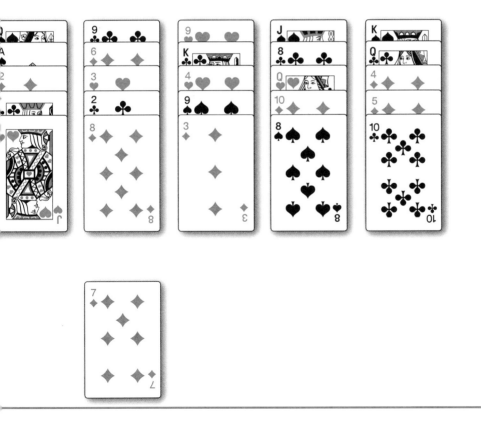

Grandfather's clock

This patience has a similar layout to Clock (see page 23), but is quite different and less mechanical.

HOW TO PLAY

Remove from the pack the ♥2, ♥6 and ♥10, the ♠3, ♠7 and ♠J, the ♦4, ♦8 and ♦Q and the ♣5, ♣9 and ♣K; arrange them on the board face up in a circle comparable to the hours on the face of a clock, with the ♣9 at noon, and the others in sequence round the dial. They serve as foundation cards to be built on in ascending, round-the-corner suit sequences until each reaches the number appropriate to its position on the dial, the Jack at 11 o'clock and the Queen at noon. (The 10, Jack, Queen and King foundations will each need four cards built on them, the others only three cards.) The remaining 40 cards are dealt face up below them, in five rows of eight cards, which for convenience may overlap (see illustration).

The cards at the bottom of the columns are available to be built on a foundation or be packed on other exposed cards, in descending, round-the-corner sequences regardless of suit. Only one card may be moved at a time, and if all the cards of one column have been moved the vacancy may be filled by any available card.

With the layout illustrated, the ♠Q may be built on the ♠J, the ♣A on the ♣K, the ♠4 on the ♠3, the ♥7 on the ♥6, the ♦9 on the ♦8, the ♦10 on the ♦9 and the ♠K on the ♠Q. The ♥Q may be packed on the ♥K, the ♦K built on the ♦Q, the ♠2 may be packed on the ♣3 and the ♦J built on the ♦10 and further plays made as the cards become exposed.

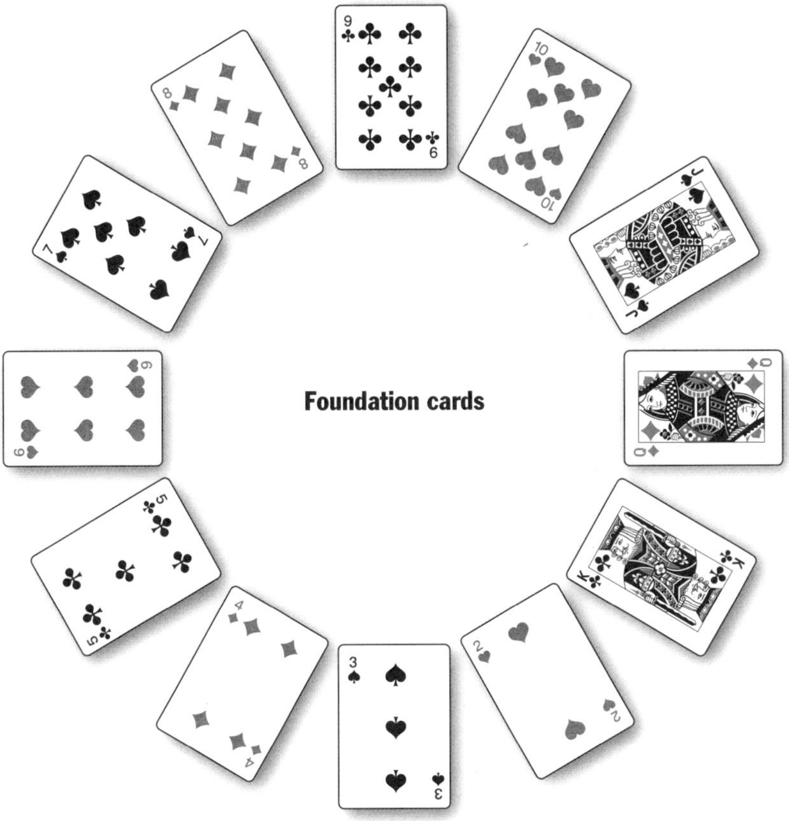
Foundation cards

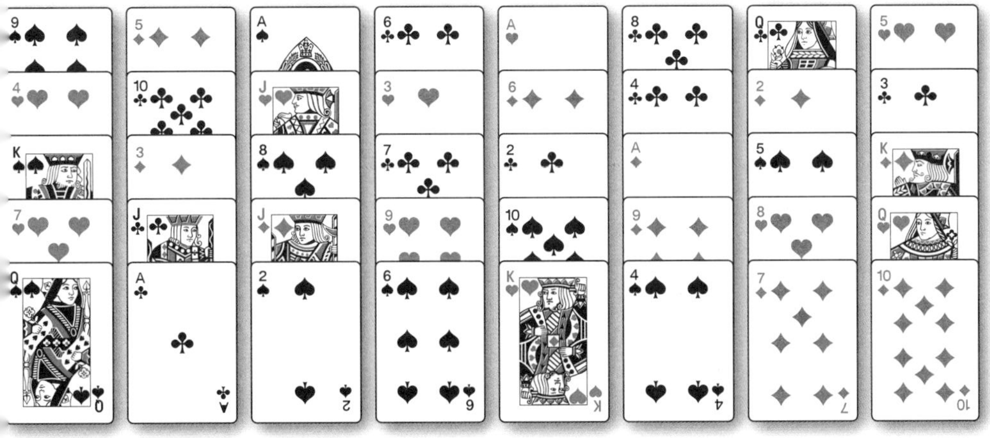

King Albert

King Albert has been given the alternative name of Idiot's Delight. Why is hard to know because Basil Dalton, an Oxford don who wrote a number of books on patience and other card games, describes it as one of the less mechanical and more intelligent games of patience. Writing in 1948 he expressed the opinion that it was quite the best single-pack game yet invented. The game is similar to Raglan (see page 48) but is rather more difficult.

HOW TO PLAY

Deal 45 cards to the board face up in rows of nine cards, then eight, seven cards, and so on, down to a single card. For convenience the cards may overlap.

The remaining seven cards, known as the reserve, may either be held in hand or placed face up on the board in front of the player (see illustration).

The object of the game is to release the Aces, play them to the centre as

Layout

foundations and build ascending suit sequences to the Kings on them.

The cards at the bottom of the columns are exposed. They may be built on the foundations, or packed on other exposed cards in descending sequences of alternating colours. Only one card may be moved at a time. A vacancy resulting from moving all the cards of a column may be filled by any available card. The cards in the reserve are available for building on a foundation or packing on the exposed cards in the layout.

In the layout illustrated, the ♠6 is packed on the ♦7, the ♣J on the ♥Q and the ♥A played to the foundation row. The ♥10 is packed on the ♣J and the ♠A played to the foundation row. The ♠9 is packed on the ♥10, the ♥8 on the ♠9, the ♠7 on the ♥8, the ♦6 on the ♠7 and the ♠5 on the ♦6. The vacancy is filled with the ♠K, the ♦4, from the reserve, is packed on the ♠5, the ♣3 on the ♦4 and the ♣A played to the foundation row and further moves made as the cards become available.

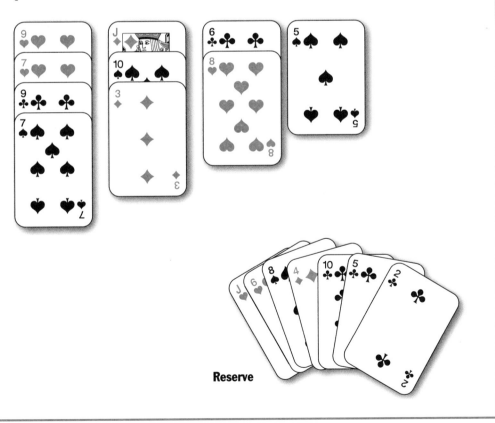

Reserve

Klondike

Demon (see page 27) and Klondike are probably the two best known and most popular one-pack patience games. In England the name of Canfield is sometimes attached to Klondike. This, however, is a misnomer, because Canfield is the name that in America is given to the patience that in England is called Demon.

HOW TO PLAY

Deal 28 cards face down in slightly overlapping rows of seven cards, then six, five, four, and so on, down to one. The bottom card of each column is turned face up (see illustration).

As they become available, the Aces are played as foundations to a row above the layout; the object of the game is to build ascending suit sequences to the Kings on the Aces.

An exposed card at the bottom of a column is available to be built on a foundation, or packed in a descending sequence of alternating colours. A sequence may be moved from one column to another only as a whole and when it can be placed in sequence, e.g. a sequence of ♦ 10, ♠ 9, ♥ 8 must be placed onto a black Jack. When an exposed card is played, the face-down card immediately above it is turned face up; when a whole column is moved, the space may be filled only by a King, either with or without a sequence attached.

The stock is dealt one card at a time to a waste heap, of which the top card is

available for building on a foundation or packing on a column in the layout. Only one deal is allowed.

The Aces must be played to the foundation row as soon as they become available, but all other cards may be left in position if the player prefers to wait in hope of finding a better move later in the game.

In the layout shown, the ♦5 is packed on the ♣6, and the card under the ♦5 is turned face up. The ♣J is packed on the ♥Q, and the ♦K moved to fill the space vacated by the ♣J. The card under the ♦K is now turned face up. Once all of the moves within the layout have been made, play from the stock can begin.

JOKER KLONDIKE

Klondike has been the subject of several variations. One of the best is Joker Klondike. It is played in the same way as the parent game, but with the Joker added to the pack. Whenever the Joker becomes available for play it must be built on a foundation as the next card in sequence. Other cards, if they are in correct sequence, are built on it, but when the natural card that it replaces becomes available it is substituted for the Joker, which is then built on another foundation.

A player may choose on which foundation to build the Joker. If it becomes available for play before a foundation has been started it must remain in its position until an Ace turns up and a foundation is started.

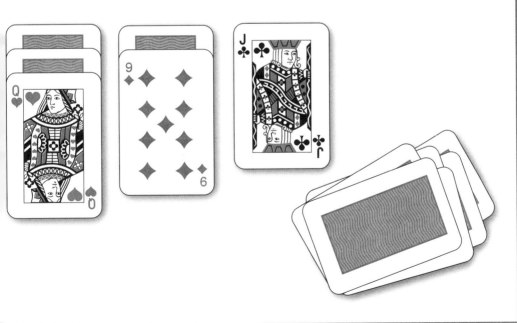

La belle Lucie

La belle Lucie, or the Fan, is one of the classic one-pack patiences; it has a very pleasing layout.

HOW TO PLAY

The entire pack is spread on the table in 17 fans of three cards and one of a single card, as illustrated.

As the Aces become available they are placed above the layout as foundations and built on in ascending suit sequences to the Kings. Only the end card of each fan and the single card are available for play. They may be built on a foundation, or packed on the end card of another fan in descending suit sequences. A space made by playing off a complete fan is not filled.

When all possible moves have been made, all of the cards not yet played to the foundations are picked up, shuffled and redealt in fans of three. If one or two cards are left over they make separate fans. Two redeals are allowed.

In the layout illustrated, the ♥A and ♣A are played to the foundation row. The ♥2 is built on the ♥A, and the ♣7 is packed on the ♣8. This releases the ♣2 that is built on the ♣A. The ♦J is packed on the ♦Q, the ♥J on the ♥Q, and the ♠A and the ♠2 go to the foundation row. After a few further moves it will become necessary to shuffle the cards and redeal.

Labyrinth

Labyrinth is quite a simple game and nothing like as tortuous as its name suggests.

HOW TO PLAY

The four Aces are played to the centre as foundation cards and built on in ascending suit sequences to the Kings. Below them eight cards are dealt face up to the board in a row. Any cards available are built on the foundations and the vacancies filled from the stock.

When all available cards have been built on the foundations and the vacancies filled, a second row of eight cards is dealt below the first. Cards from it are built on the foundations, but the vacancies are not filled: this only happens in the first row.

Dealing and building on the foundations is continued in this way until the stock is exhausted.

The cards in both the top and bottom rows are exposed and built on the foundations. When a card is played from the top row the card below it becomes exposed, and when one is played from the bottom row the card above it becomes exposed. As only vacancies in the first row are filled, during the game there may be a number of unfilled vacancies in the layout (see illustration). It may suggest a labyrinth.

The game succeeds if all four foundations are built up to the Kings. Only one deal is allowed, and if the game has not been won when the stock has been exhausted, the player has the grace of playing any one card from the layout to a foundation.

In the illustration, the ♠3 is built on the ♠2, the ♥4 on the ♥3 exposing the ♠4, which is built on the ♠3. The ♥5 is built on the ♥4, the ♥6 on the ♥5, the ♥7 on the ♥6, and the ♥8 on the ♥7. Once all the available moves have been made, the holes in the top row are filled, another row of cards is dealt at the bottom and play continues as before.

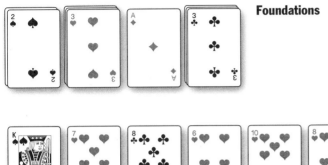

Foundations

Layout

Little spider

HOW TO PLAY

The red Aces and black Kings (or the black Aces and red Kings) are placed in a row on the table to serve as foundations. Then eight cards are dealt, face up, in two rows of four cards, one above the foundation cards, the other below them, as illustrated.

The object of the game is to build on the Aces ascending suit sequences to the Kings, and descending suit sequences on the Kings to the Aces.

During the deal (i.e. after each round of eight cards), cards from the upper row may be built on any of the four foundation cards, but a card from the lower row may be built only on the foundation card directly above it.

After all six batches of eight cards have been dealt, the top cards of all eight piles are playable and may be built on any foundation cards or packed on any other pile in the layout. The piles are packed in ascending or descending continuous sequences (an Ace ranks below a 2 and above a King) regardless of suit. A space made by removing an entire pile is not filled.

In the layout illustrated, which shows the game after all the cards have been dealt (as happens rarely, no cards were played to the foundations during the deal), the ♣Q may be built on the ♣K and the ♥2 on the ♥A. The ♣10 may be packed on the ♠J, and the ♣5 on the ♠6. The cards exposed by these moves may then be played, if possible.

Martha

HOW TO PLAY

Remove the Aces from the pack and play them to the centre as foundation cards. Deal the rest of the pack in 12 columns of four cards, the first and third cards of each column face down, the second and fourth face up. The rows may overlap for convenience (see illustration).

The object of the game is to build on the Aces ascending suit sequences to the Kings.

The bottom cards of the columns are available to be built on the foundations, or packed on the exposed cards in the layout in descending sequences of alternating colours. Provided the order and alternating colours are retained a

Foundations

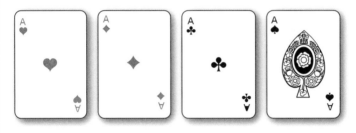

Layout

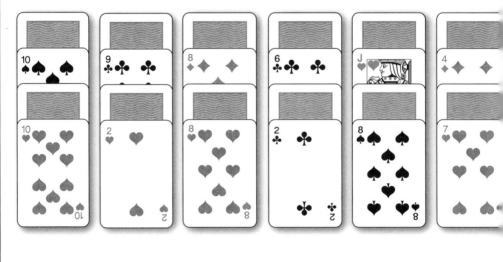

sequence may be moved either wholly or in part from one column to another. Vacancies in the layout, however, may be filled only by a single card. The face-down cards in the layout are turned face up when the cards below them have been played.

In the layout, the ♥2 is built on the ♥A and the face-down card turned. The ♣2 is built on the ♣A and the face-down card turned. The ♠9 is packed on the ♥10, the ♥8 on the ♠9, the ♣7 on the ♥8 and the face-down cards turned after each move. Not knowing where almost half of the cards are makes this game a good challenge.

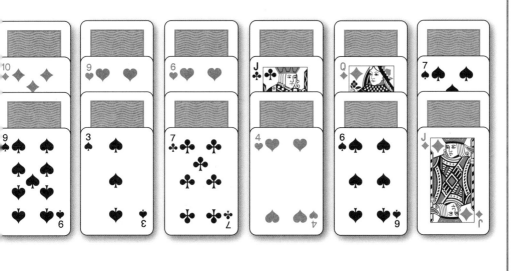

Maze

Maze is an excellent form of patience because some skill is necessary if it is to be successful.

HOW TO PLAY

The 52 cards of the pack are dealt face up in two rows of eight cards, and four of nine cards (see illustration).

The four Kings are then discarded. This leaves four spaces, or six in all, because as well as the spaces left by the discard of the Kings, the spaces at the end of the first and second rows are taken into the layout for the play (see illustration opposite).

The object of the game is to arrange the 48 cards in four ascending suit sequences, from Aces to Queens, beginning with an Ace at the extreme left of the top row and ending with a Queen at the extreme right of the bottom row. The sequences read from left to right and continue from the end of one row to the beginning of the next. Only one card may be moved at a time.

The rules for moving a card into a space are:

The card must be in suit sequence one higher than the card to the left of the space or one lower than the card to the right of the space
The bottom and top rows are continuous
When a space occurs to the right of a Queen it may be filled with either an Ace or a card one lower in suit sequence than the card to the right of the space

Suppose the layout is as in the illustration. After the four Kings have been discarded, the space left vacant by the ♥K may be filled by any Ace, or with the ♠9 (by reason of the ♠10 on the right of the space) or the ♠8 (by reason of the ♠7 at the end of the bottom row). The space at the extreme right of the top row may be filled either with the ♥2 or ♥4, that at the extreme right of the second row either with the ♥10 or ♠10. The space left vacant by the ♦K may be filled either with the ♣Q or ♠5.

To begin the game, play the ♠A to the top left corner of the layout, and the ♥10 to its vacant place. Play the ♦5 to the left of the ♦6 in the top row, and the ♦J to the left of the ♦Q in the bottom row. Play the ♠10 to the extreme right of the second row, and the ♠2 followed by the ♠3 to the right of the ♠A in the top row. Play the ♠5 to the left of the ♠6, the ♣J to the left of the ♣Q and the ♠4 to the left of the ♠5. The ♥5 is played to the left of the ♥6, the ♥9 to the left of the ♥10 and the ♠9 to the left of the ♠10. Now the ♦5 in the top row may be played to the right of the ♦4 and the ♠4 to the right of the ♠3 in the top row. With the ♠A, ♠2, ♠3 and ♠4 in position, the game is progressing well.

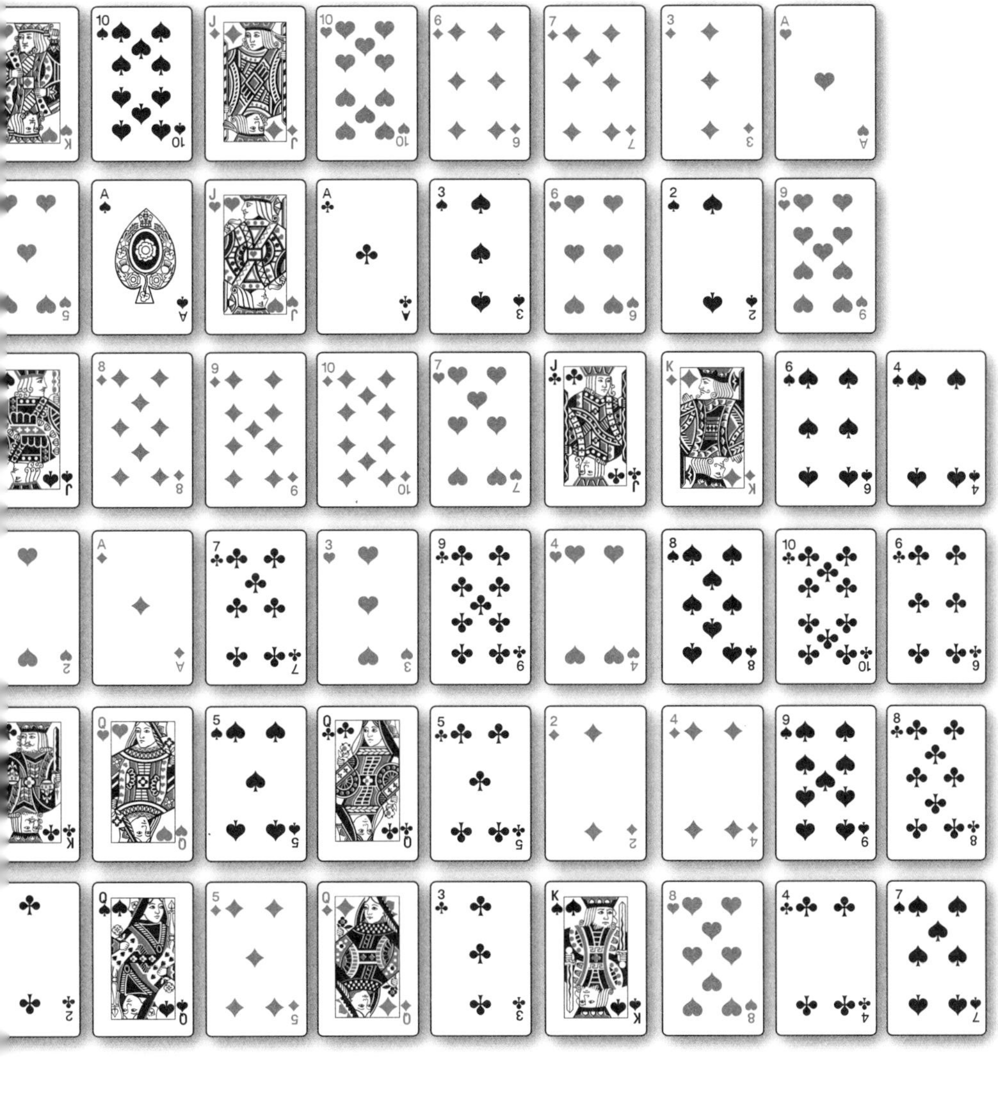

Monte Carlo

Monte Carlo, Weddings or Double or Quits is a rather simple patience that calls for very little skill.

HOW TO PLAY

First, 20 cards are dealt face up to the board in four rows of five cards (see illustration 1).

The object of the game is to discard the whole pack. Any two cards of the same rank that touch each other, at top or bottom, to either side or diagonally,

are discarded. The layout is then consolidated by first closing up the top row from right to left and then bringing up, in order, cards from the left-hand side of the next row, and continuing this process until there are no gaps between the cards. The vacancies in the lower rows can then be filled with cards from the stock.

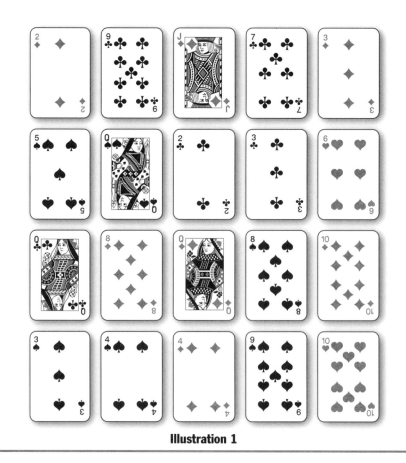

Illustration 1

If three cards of the same rank touch each other the player chooses which two to discard. It is best to discard the pair that will give more additional plays after the layout has been consolidated.

The game is won if the whole pack is discarded. It's fun even though the odds are against you, and if no pair touches in the first 20 cards the game is lost before it started.

In the original layout in illustration 1 (see below left), the ♦3 may be discarded with the ♣3, the ♠Q either

with the ♣Q or ♦Q. (It is better discarded with the ♦Q to bring the ♦8 and ♠8 together after consolidation.) The ♦10 is discarded with the ♥10 and the ♠4 with the ♦4.

When the remaining cards have been moved up, the situation is as in illustration 2 (see below), and the three vacancies in the third row and the five in the fourth row should now be filled from the stock and the game continued.

Illustration 2

Puss in the corner

HOW TO PLAY

Remove the four Aces and play them in a square in the centre of the board. They serve as foundations for building in ascending colour (not necessarily suit) sequences to the Kings. Four cards are dealt to the board to begin waste heaps, and they are placed at the corners of the foundation square (see illustration).

Four cards are dealt, one at a time, from the stock and played on any of the waste heaps (not necessarily one on each waste heap – you could put two, three or four on the same one if you wish). The top cards of the waste heaps are available to be built on the foundations.

Continue dealing in this way – building available cards on the foundations after each deal of four cards has been made – until the stock is exhausted.

Only one redeal is allowed. The waste heaps may be picked up in any order and redealt without shuffling.

In the illustration, the ♠2 may be built either on the ♠A or ♣A. High cards dealt from the stock should be played on the ♦J.

TACTICS

It is best to keep one waste heap for high cards and, whenever possible, play a card on a higher rather than a lower one.

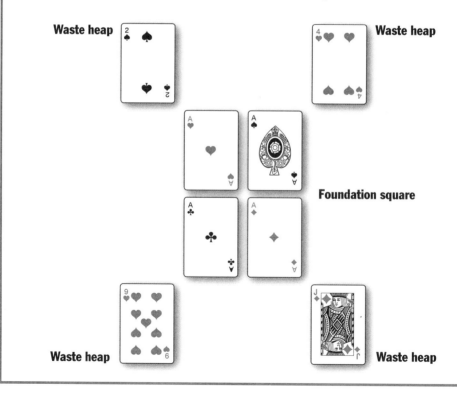

Waste heap   Waste heap

Foundation square

Waste heap   Waste heap

Pyramid

Pyramid, or Pile of Twenty-eight, is an interesting form of patience, and not an easy one, having one chance of succeeding in about 50 games.

HOW TO PLAY

First, 28 cards are dealt face up to the board in seven rows, beginning with one card and adding one per row so the seventh row contains seven cards. The cards should be arranged in the form of a pyramid, so that every card (except those in the bottom row) will be overlapped by two cards in the row below it. The removal of two adjacent cards in a row exposes one card in the row above.

The object of the game is to discard the whole pack. Kings are discarded singly, but all other cards are discarded in a pair whose pips add to 13 (Queens counting as 12 and Jacks as 11). Only exposed cards may be discarded.

The stock is turned card by card to a waste heap, the top card of which is exposed and can be paired with an exposed card or the next dealt from stock.

In the layout illustrated, the ♠K is discarded; the ♣7 and ♣6 are paired and discarded; the ♠10 and ♣3 (from the waste heap) are paired and discarded; the ♦10 and ♠3 are paired and discarded. As no further discards can be made, the next card of the stock is dealt to the waste heap. And so on.

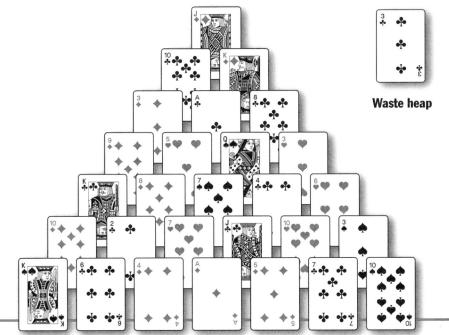

Waste heap

Raglan

HOW TO PLAY

The four Aces are placed in a row in the centre of the table as foundations. Below them, 42 cards are dealt, face up, in seven, slightly overlapping rows; the first of nine cards, the second of eight, and so on down to a row of three cards. The remaining six cards (the stock) are placed face up in a row below the layout (see illustration).

The object of the game is to build on the Aces ascending suit sequences to the Kings.

The bottom cards of the columns, and the six cards in the stock, are exposed. They may be built on a foundation, and those at the bottom of a column (but not those in the stock) may be packed in descending sequences of alternating colours. Cards must be moved singly

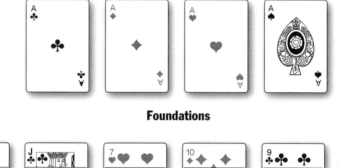

Foundations

Layout

and sequences may not be moved. When all the cards of a column have been removed, the player may fill the space with any exposed card.

In the layout illustrated, the ♦5 is packed on the ♠6, and the ♠3 on the ♥4 that has been left exposed by the play of the ♦5. The ♥Q, in the stock, may be packed on the ♠K, and the ♠10 on the ♦J. Now the ♥9 may be packed on the ♠10. The ♠4 in the stock is packed on the ♦5, the ♦3 on the ♠4 and the ♥6 on the ♣7. The space is filled by the ♣Q, the ♣2 is played to its foundation, the ♠J is packed on the ♥Q, the ♠8 on the ♥9 and the ♦10 on the ♠J. The ♠9 is packed on the ♦10, the ♥8 on the ♠9,

and ♦6 is played to the space and the ♠2 followed by the ♠3 are built on their foundation. The space is filled with the ♥4, the ♣5 is packed on the ♦6 and the ♥4 on the ♣5. The ♦7 and the ♣6 from the stock are packed on the ♠8, the ♥5 on the ♣6 and the space is filled with the ♦9. Now the ♥2, ♥3, ♥4, ♥5, ♥6 and ♥7 are built on their foundation. The ♣7 is packed on the ♥8, the space is filled with the ♠7, and the ♦2 and ♦3 are built on their foundation, followed by the ♠4 and ♠5 on theirs. Although the ♣3 and ♣4 are badly placed the game has progressed well, and there is every chance that it will succeed.

Stock

Scorpion

HOW TO PLAY

Seven cards, four face down and three face up, are dealt in a row. Two more rows are dealt in the same way, and then four rows of face-up cards. For convenience the rows may overlap slightly (see illustration). The remaining three cards are temporarily set aside.

Leaving the four Kings within the layout, the object of the game is to build descending suit sequences to the Aces on them.

The cards at the bottom of the columns are exposed, and they may be packed with the next lower cards in suit sequence. To do this a card may be taken from anywhere in the layout, but if a card is not taken from the bottom of a column, all the cards below it in the column must be taken with it.

In the layout shown, the ♦3 may be packed on the ♦4, but the ♣2 must go with it. In the same way, the ♠5 may be packed on the ♠6, but the ♠7, ♥6, ♣A and ♦10 must be moved with it. Nothing, of course, is packed on an Ace.

When a face-down card is cleared, it is turned face up, and when a whole column is cleared the space is filled by a King, together with any cards below it in the column from which it is taken.

When no further moves can be made, the three cards, temporarily set aside, are

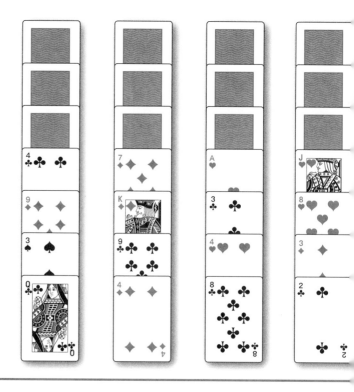

now dealt face up, one to the foot of each of the three columns at the extreme left of the layout.

The game is by no means an easy one and calls for some care and forethought if it is to succeed.

As a start, the layout should be inspected closely. If there is a reverse sequence, such as ♦Q, ♦J, ♦K, in one column the game can never be won; nor can it if there is a 'criss-cross', such as the ♠9 on the ♦6 in one column and the ♦5 on the ♠10 in another. In such cases as these it is a waste of time to continue.

If the layout offers promise of success, the first move should be an attempt to uncover the face-down cards. In the

layout illustrated, for example, it will be seen that the ♣4, together with the ♦9, ♠3 and ♣Q, will free a face-down card if the combination is packed on the ♣5. The first move, therefore, is to pack the ♠5, together with the ♠7, ♥6, ♣A and ♦10, on the ♠6.

TACTICS

Careful thought should always be given to a situation before a move is made. Carelessness may well end in the player blocking the game.

Simple Simon

HOW TO PLAY

Deal the whole pack face up to the board in eight rows (which may overlap), the first row of ten cards, the second of nine, etc. down to a row of three cards (see illustration).

The object of the game is to build, within the layout, descending suit sequences from the exposed Kings to the Aces.

The bottom card of each column (other than a King) may be packed in a descending sequence regardless of suit and colour. Only one card may be moved at a time, except that a sequence may be moved as a whole if it consists of cards all of one suit.

A vacancy left by the removal of all the cards from a column may be filled by any exposed card or by a sequence if all the cards are of one suit.

This is an excellent game, but the name given to it is a mystery because it is far from easy or simple.

In the layout illustrated, the ♣Q may be built on the ♣K, the ♠10 may be packed on the ♠J, the ♥9 on the ♠10, and the ♠9 on the ♦10.

Now, the ♦6 may be packed on the ♥7, the ♥5 on the ♦6, and the vacancy filled with the ♠K. The ♠Q may be built on the ♠K, and the vacancy filled with the ♣K and ♣Q in sequence.

Sir Tommy

No one knows, and probably no one ever will know, which is the original patience from which all of the others were derived. This one, which is sometimes known as Try Again or Old Patience, may be it. Certainly, the game could hardly be simpler.

HOW TO PLAY

The cards are dealt face up one by one, and played at the discretion of the player to four waste heaps (see illustration). As they occur, the Aces are played to a foundation row and built on in ascending sequences, regardless of suits and colour, to the Kings.

After television, it's the best time-waster known.

In the game in progress as illustrated, two Aces have been played to the foundation row and then built on.

Suppose the next card from the stock is the ♥A; it is played to the foundation row and the ♣2 built on it.

TACTICS

The top cards of the waste heaps are available to be played to the foundations but, as there is only the one deal, and a card may not be transferred from one waste heap to another, the best that can be done is to reserve one waste heap on which to play the Kings and hope that they will show up early in the game.

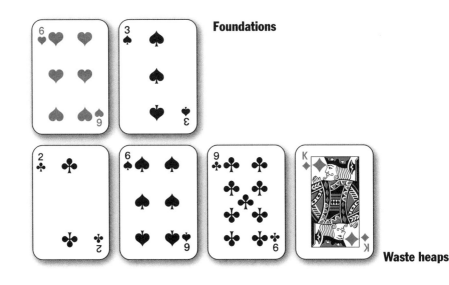

Foundations

Waste heaps

Six by six

Six by Six is a simple building-up patience that may not be as well known as it deserves to be.

HOW TO PLAY

First, 36 cards are dealt face up to the board in six overlapping rows (see illustration).

The object of the game is to release the Aces, play them to the centre as foundation cards, then to build on them in ascending suit sequences to the Kings.

The bottom card of each column is exposed. It may be built on a foundation, or packed on an exposed card in the layout in descending sequence regardless of suit and colour. Provided the order is retained, a sequence may be moved, either wholly or in part, from the foot of one column to that of another. When all the cards of a column have been played,

the vacancy may be filled by any exposed card or by a sequence.

The stock is dealt one card at a time, and any card that cannot be built on a foundation or packed on the layout, is played to the foot of the left-hand column. Only one deal is allowed.

In the layout illustrated, the ♦A is played to the centre and the ♦2 built on it. The ♣A is played to the centre. The ♣5 is packed on the ♥6. The ♥J is packed on the ♣Q, the ♥10 on the ♥J, the ♣9 on the ♥10, the ♠8 on the ♣9, the ♥7 on the ♠8 and the ♦6 on the ♥7. The ♥A is played to the centre and the ♥2 built on it. Once no more moves can be made within the layout, cards can start being dealt from the stock.

Stone-wall

HOW TO PLAY

Deal 36 cards to the board in six rows of six cards: the first, third and fifth rows face down, the second, fourth and sixth rows face up. For convenience the rows may overlap. The stock (16 cards in all) may either be held in hand or spread face up on the table (see illustration).

Any Aces in the stock, or exposed in the sixth row of the layout, are moved to a foundation row, to be built on in ascending suit sequences up to the Kings.

Exposed cards in the bottom row of the layout are packed in descending sequences of alternating colours, either with cards from the stock or exposed cards in the layout. A sequence may be transferred either as a whole or in part to an exposed card, this maintains the order and alternating colours. When a card or sequence is removed from immediately below a face-down card, the card is turned face up and is available for play.

When all the cards in a column have been moved, the vacancy may be filled with either an exposed card or sequence from the layout or a card from the stock.

The game is by no means a difficult one, but success comes only if there is a favourable run of cards. Vacancies in the top row of the layout are very helpful.

In the layout illustrated, the ♥A from the stock and the ♠A in the sixth row of the layout are moved to a foundation row, and the card immediately above the ♠A is turned face up. Suppose it is the ♣4. Now the ♥7 from the stock may be packed on the ♠8, the ♠6 from the stock on the ♥7 and the ♦5 from the stock on the ♠6. The ♣4 may be packed on the ♦5, the ♦J on the ♠Q and the card immediately above the ♦J turned face up.

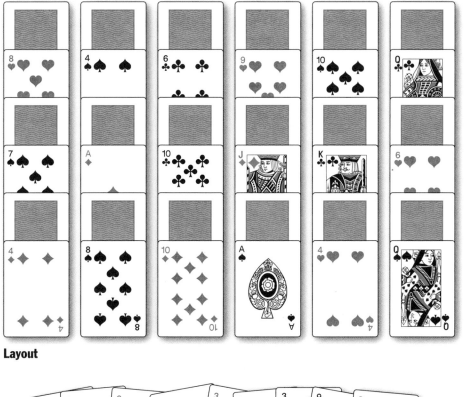

Layout

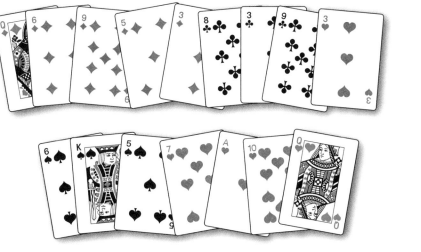

Stock

Three blind mice

This is a simple patience that more or less operates itself. This one does not turn out very often (about one time in ten) and has a way of getting stuck very near the end, which you may find amusing or aggravating depending on your temperament.

HOW TO PLAY

Five rows of ten cards are dealt out, overlapping so that the faces can be seen, as shown in the illustration. The cards in the seven columns to the left should be placed face up, but the three cards in the top three rows of the three right-hand columns should be face down and the two odd cards kept on one side to be played whenever it becomes possible to do so.

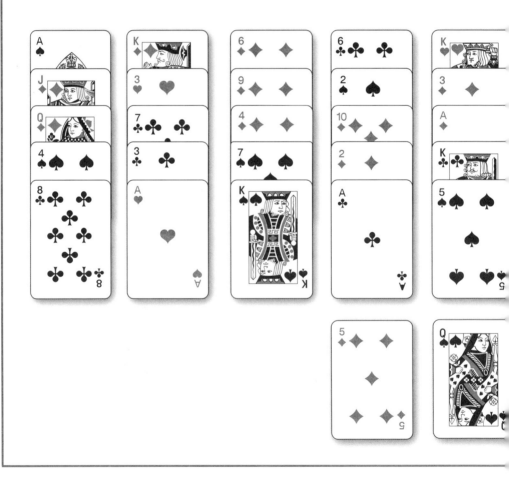

The object is to build the four suits in descending sequence (Queen on King, 8 on 9, and so on) from King down to Ace. For this game, only the exposed cards can be built onto, but the card doing the building can be anywhere except farther up the same column, so long as it is face up. If there are other cards below the one being built, they are carried with it.

When one of the 'blind' cards is exposed it is turned over and can join in the play.

Kings may be played into the vacancies that arise when one of the ten columns becomes empty.

The illustration shows the start of a game. The ♠Q may be played onto the ♠K, but the ♦5 has to wait until the ♦6 is exposed. The building might start with the ♣7 being played on the ♣8, keeping the ♣3 and ♥A with of it. This exposes the ♥3, so the ♥2 (and ♦7) can be built on the ♥3. Now one of the blind cards is exposed and should be turned over.

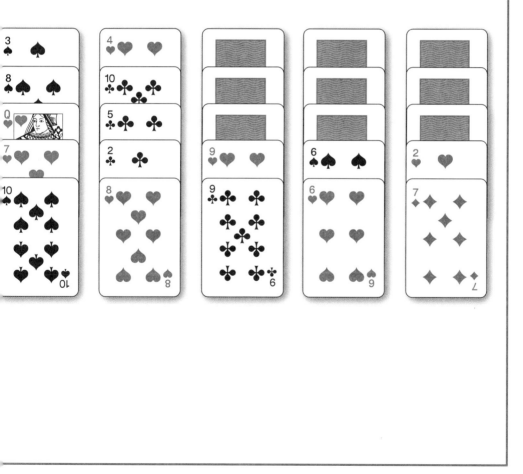

Tower of Hanoy

This patience game is based on a toy invented by a French mathematician in 1883, and still to be found. It consists of three pegs on a board, on one of which is a tower of eight discs with holes in the centre. The discs are of different diameters, and are stacked from the largest at the foot to the smallest at the top. The object of the game is, by moving discs between the pegs, to transfer the tower to either of the other pegs, one disc at a time, but never placing a larger disc on top of a smaller one. It can be done in 255 moves. The playing card version will usually be achieved in far fewer.

HOW TO PLAY

Remove from the pack the Ace to 9 (inclusive) of any one suit, and, after shuffling them, deal them to the board face up in three rows of three cards (see illustration 1, bottom right).

The object of the game is to arrange the cards in a descending sequence in one column with the 9 at the top and the Ace at the bottom. The movement of the cards is governed by four rules:

Only one card may be moved at a time

Only the bottom card of a column may be moved

A card may be moved only to the bottom of another column and below a higher-denomination card

When all the cards in a column have been moved, the vacancy may be filled by the bottom card of either of the other two columns

With the layout in illustration 1, the skilful player will play first to get the 9 to the top of a column, so the ♥2 should be played below the ♥9, the ♥4 below the ♥8, then the ♥2 below the ♥4, the ♥A below the ♥2 and the ♥9 to the middle column.

This results in the situation in illustration 2 with the ♥9 in position, the next step is to get the ♥8 below it, the ♥7 below the ♥8, and so on. The moves continue: the ♥A below the ♥6, the ♥2 below the ♥9, the ♥A below the ♥2, the ♥4 below the ♥6, with the lower-value cards switching back and forth between columns to expose the higher-denomination ones in turn. Provided the player perseveres, success is assured.

Illustration 2

Illustration 1

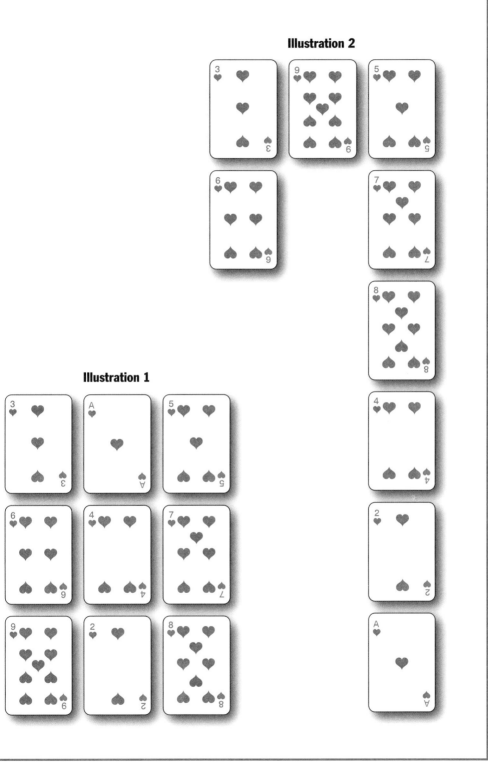

Vacancies

Vacancies is more usually known as Gaps, and sometimes as Spaces. Whatever the name, the game is an excellent one with the merit that it is one of the few patience games in which the lucky order of the cards is less important than the player's skill. At every move the player is faced with four vacancies to fill, but can only fill one of them and any move releases another card, so much depends on the order in which the vacancies are filled.

HOW TO PLAY

The whole pack is dealt face up to the board in four rows of 13 cards, and the Aces are discarded leaving four vacancies (see illustration).

The object of the game is to arrange the cards so that every row consists of one suit in sequential order, with the 2 on the extreme left and the King on the extreme right. The player decides which row he will allocate to each suit, and,

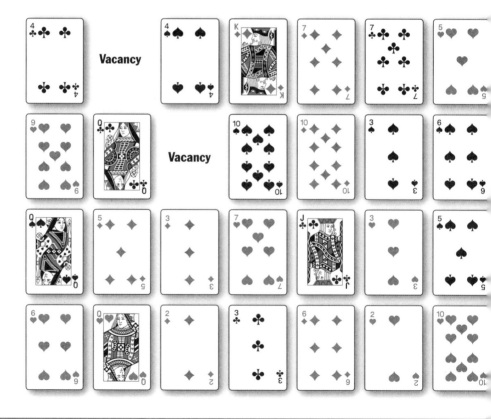

having decided, must stand by this order throughout the game.

A vacancy may be filled only by the card that is next higher in rank and of the same suit as the card on the left of the vacancy. Obviously, filling a vacancy leaves another vacancy to be filled and this is done in the same way until the run of the game is brought to a halt by the position of the four Kings.

Three deals are permitted. When no further moves can be made after the first deal, all the cards that are not in their final positions are picked up, shuffled, and the layout remade by dealing them to the board, leaving a vacancy in each row to the immediate right of the cards that are in sequence. If a row has no cards in sequence then the vacancy is left on the extreme left of the row.

In the deal as illustrated, the ♠6 is played to the right of the ♠5, and the ♠4 to the right of the ♠3. The ♣5 is played to the right of the ♣4, and the ♣6 to the right of the ♣5.

The ♠Q is played to the right of the ♠J and the player is now in a position to begin the third row by playing the 2 of the suit chosen for that row into the vacancy left by the ♠Q.

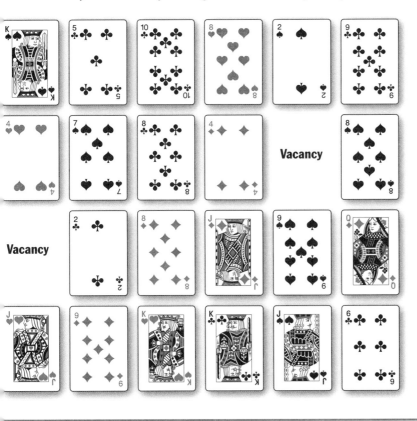

Westcliff

This game is one of the standard patiences that is neither too difficult nor too easy. With care the practised player should be able to win eight or nine games out of every ten.

HOW TO PLAY

First, 30 cards are dealt to the board in three rows of ten cards. The first and second row are dealt face down, the third row face up (see illustration 1, top). As they become available, the Aces are played to the centre as foundation cards, to be built on in ascending suit sequences to the Kings.

The exposed cards of the layout may be packed in descending sequences of alternating colours, and any face-up card or sequence may be packed on another face-up card or sequence in the layout, provided that the sequential order is

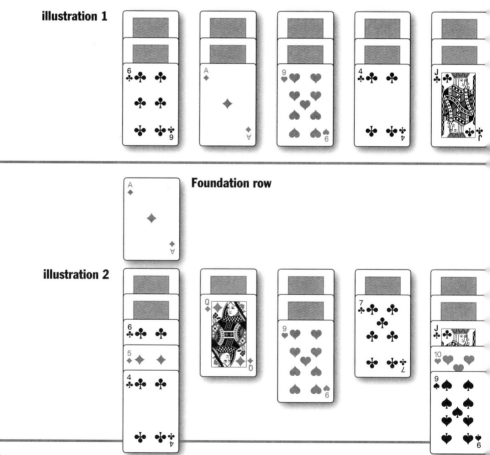

illustration 1

Foundation row

illustration 2

retained. When a face-down card is released, because a card or sequence below it is moved, it is turned face up and becomes available for play.

The stock is dealt one card at a time and any card that cannot be played to a foundation or to the layout is played to a waste heap, the top card of which is always available. Only one deal is permitted.

A vacancy in the layout, resulting from all of the cards in a column being moved, may be filled with either a card from the waste heap or a card or sequence from a column in the layout.

If the deal is as in illustration 1, the ♦A is played to the centre and the card above it turned face up; the ♥10 is packed on the ♣J, the ♠9 on the ♥10, the ♦5 on the ♣6, and the ♣4 on the ♦5.

The cards in the second row released by moving the ♥10, ♠9, ♦5 and ♣4 are turned face up (see illustration 2, bottom). Now the ♦6 is packed on the ♣7, the ♠5 on the ♦6, and the ♣Q on the ♦K. The cards in the top row released by moving the ♦6, ♠5 and ♣Q are turned face up. Once no more moves are available, cards may be dealt from the stock.

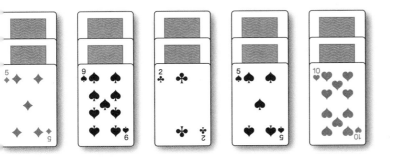

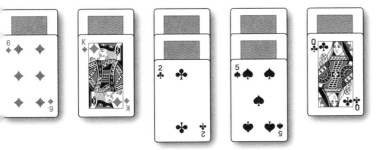

Above and below

HOW TO PLAY

Deal eight piles of 11 cards face up to the board; then deal 16 cards face up, one above and one below each pile (see illustration).

The object of the game is to release an Ace and a King of each suit, play them to the centre as foundations, and build on the Aces ascending suit sequences to the Kings, and descending suit sequences on the Kings to the Aces.

The top cards of the piles may be built on the foundations, or packed on the cards in the two rows above and below them, either in ascending or descending suit sequences, the direction of which may be reversed at any time. The cards in the rows may be built on the

foundations, or packed on each other in ascending or descending suit sequences. Cards may be moved only singly.

A vacancy in a row must be filled by the top card of the pile immediately above or below it, and when all the cards of a pile have been played, the vacancy must be filled by the top card of the pile to its right or left.

With the layout as shown, the ♦A is played to the foundation row and the ♠Q fills the vacancy. The ♣K is played to the foundation row and the vacancy is filled by the ♦J, the ♣Q is built on the ♣K and the vacancy filled with the ♥10. The ♥7 is packed on the ♥8, the ♣10 fills the vacancy and the ♣9 is packed on the ♣10. The ♠7 is packed on the ♠6 and the ♣2 fills the vacancy.

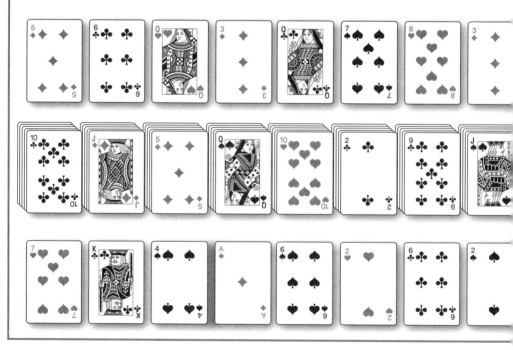

Alhambra

HOW TO PLAY

Remove one Ace and King of each suit and play them to the centre as foundation cards. Below them deal face up 32 cards in eight piles of four cards each (see illustration).

The object of the game is to build on the Aces ascending suit sequences to the Kings, and descending suit sequences to the Aces on the Kings.

The stock is dealt one card at a time and any card that cannot be built on a foundation is played to a waste heap, the top card of which is available to be built on a foundation.

The top cards of the eight piles may be built on the foundations, or they may be packed on the top card of the waste heap either in ascending or in descending, round-the-corner suit sequences. A vacancy created by playing all four cards of a pile is not filled. The stock may be dealt three times in all.

With the deal as illustrated, the ♦Q is built on the ♦K, and the ♠2 on the ♠A. The player has the option of packing either the ♥10 or the ♥8 on the ♥9, the top card of the waste heap.

oundations

ckets

Waste heap

Alternation

HOW TO PLAY

First, 49 cards are dealt to the board in seven overlapping rows: the first, third, fifth and seventh rows face up, the others face down (see illustration).

The object of the game is to release the eight Aces, play them to the centre as foundation cards and build on them ascending suit sequences to the Kings.

The bottom cards of the columns are exposed. They may be built on the foundations, or packed on other exposed cards in the layout in descending sequences of alternating colours. Provided the sequential order is retained, a sequence may be moved, either as a whole or in part, from one column to another. When the play of a card or sequence results in a face-down card

Layout

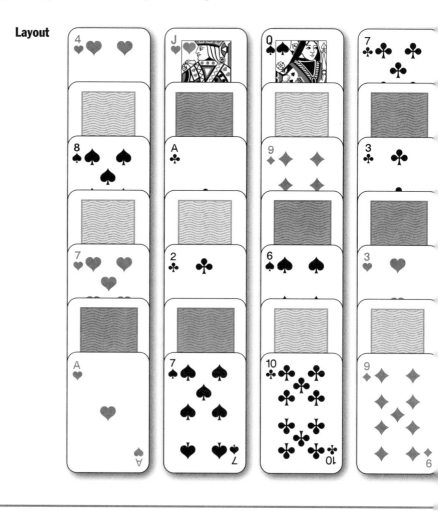

being exposed it is turned face up. A vacancy may be filled by any exposed card or sequence.

The stock is dealt one card at a time, and any card that cannot be built on a foundation or packed on the layout is played to a waste heap. There is only one deal.

With the cards as dealt in the illustration, the ♥A is played to the foundation row, the ♦9 is packed on the ♣10 and the ♣8 on the ♦9; the ♦6 is packed on the ♠7. The face-down cards are turned face up. When no further moves can be made the first card of the stock is dealt.

Stock

Babette

HOW TO PLAY

A row of eight cards is dealt face up to the board. The object of the game is to play one Ace and one King of each suit to a foundation row, and build on the Aces ascending suit sequences to the Kings, and descending suit sequences to the Aces on the Kings. All of the available cards are played to a foundation row, then further rows of eight cards are dealt below the first, and the foundations built on in the same way, until all the stock is exhausted.

A card is only exposed and available to be played to a foundation when its lower edge is free. No other card is available to be played, and vacancies that occur by playing cards from the rows to the foundations are not filled (see illustration).

One redeal is allowed. When the stock is exhausted, the cards remaining in each column are slid into packets, which are picked up from left to right to remake the pack.

In the illustration, the third row has just been dealt. The ♠Q, ♠3 and all eight cards in the third row are exposed. The ♠2 may be built on the ♠A, but the ♠3 should not be built on the ♠2; it is better to wait until the other ♠3 is dealt. The ♣Q should be built on the ♣K.

Foundations

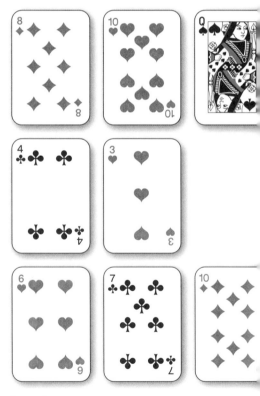

Layout

TACTICS

Unless it becomes necessary to release an important card in a higher row, it is unwise to play a card from above a vacancy until its duplicate has been dealt; the game is often lost if the right card is not chosen to be played.

Big Bertha

HOW TO PLAY

Deal 90 cards face up to the board in six overlapping rows of 15 cards. The remaining 14 cards are retained in the hand or spread on the table in front of the player as a reserve (see illustration).

The object of the game is to release the Aces, play them to the centre as foundation cards and build ascending suit sequences to the Queen (Big Bertha) on them. The Kings are taken out of the game as they become exposed.

The bottom cards of the columns and the cards in the reserve are exposed and may be built on the foundations. The bottom cards of the columns may also be packed on each other in descending sequences of alternating colours. Provided the order and alternation of colour are retained a sequence may be moved from the foot of one column to another.

Layout

A vacancy in the layout, when all the cards of a column have been played, may be filled with a sequence or an exposed card.

In the layout illustrated the ♥K and ♦K are taken out of the game. The ♦A, ♠A and ♣A are played to the centre, and the ♠2 built on the ♠A and the ♣2 on the ♣A. The ♦5 is packed on the ♠6 and the ♠K taken out of the game. The ♣4 can then be packed on the ♦5, the

♥A played to the centre and the ♣K taken out of the game.

TACTICS

When both duplicates of a card are available, the player should ascertain which will be more useful.

Reserve

British square

British Square is a building patience with the unusual feature that the foundations are built first in ascending sequences and then in descending ones.

HOW TO PLAY

First, 16 cards are dealt face up to the board in four overlapping rows of four cards. One Ace of each suit is played to the centre as it becomes available to serve as a foundation. These are built on in ascending suit sequences to the Kings, then the duplicate Kings are placed on the foundations and built on in descending suit sequences to the Aces.

The bottom card of a column may be built on a foundation, or may be packed on each other either in ascending or descending suit sequence. Only one card may be moved at a time, and the first card packed on a column dictates the direction of a sequence, which cannot be reversed by later cards. However, the player may alter the direction of a sequence by reversing it onto an available card at the foot of another column. An ascending sequence ends with a King, a descending one with an Ace. A vacancy is filled either by a card from the stock or from the waste heap (see illustration).

The stock is turned one card at a time, and any card that cannot be built on a foundation or packed on the layout is played to a waste heap, the top card of which is always available to be played. There is no second deal.

The illustration shows a game in progress. The Aces have been played to the centre as foundation cards, the ♣A built up to the ♣3, and the ♠A to the ♠2. The ♣8 is packed on the ♣9 because the ♣10 packed on the ♣J dictates a descending sequence. The ♠3 is built on the ♠2, releasing the ♥8. The ♥8, however, may not be packed on the ♥9 because the ♥9 packed on the ♥8 dictates an ascending sequence.

TACTICS

The foundations are first built on in ascending sequences and then in descending ones, so a duplicate card in the layout of one already in a foundation should be packed on in the opposite direction, otherwise it will be impossible to play the sequence to the foundation.

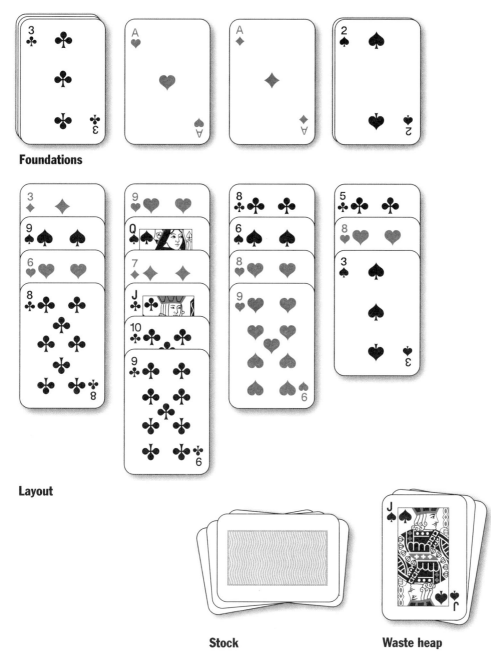

Foundations

Layout

Stock

Waste heap

Capricious

Capricious is a classic game also called Capricieuse.

HOW TO PLAY

Play an Ace and a King of each suit to the centre as foundations. Below them deal 12 cards face up to the board. These may be arranged in any way that is convenient to the player; three rows of four cards each is as good as any (see illustration).

The object of the game is to build ascending suit sequences on the Aces to the Kings, and descending suit sequences on the Kings to the Aces.

As the cards are being dealt to the original layout, any that may be built onto a foundation are built immediately – they do not go into the layout. Once a card has been placed in the layout, it cannot be played to a foundation until the whole pack has been dealt. Once the 12 cards are in position, they form the bases of 12 piles. Return to the beginning and continue dealing cards onto the 12 piles in turn, always playing a card to a foundation if possible. Do not miss out any piles (i.e. if a card is played to a foundation instead of a pile in the layout, the following card is played to that pile).

When the whole pack has been dealt, the top cards of the 12 piles are available not only to be built on the foundations but to be packed on each other in ascending or descending suit sequences.

Sequences in the layout are not round-the-corner (only a Queen may be packed on a King and a 2 on an Ace) but reversing the direction of a sequence on the same pile is permitted. Two

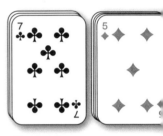

Foundations

redeals are allowed. To remake the pack, the piles are picked up in the reverse order to which they were dealt.

The game in the illustration is well advanced. The foundations have been built up during the deal. The ♠2 is packed on the ♠A and the ♣2 on the ♣3 or, if preferred, the ♣3 on the ♣2. The cards under those that have been moved are then available to be played.

Layout

Colorado

Colorado is a fairly simple game that should succeed about five times out of six.

HOW TO PLAY

Deal 20 cards face up to the board in two rows of ten cards. As they become available, play to the centre one Ace and one King of each suit as foundations (see illustration).

The object of the game is to build on the Aces ascending suit sequences to the Kings, and descending suit sequences on the Kings to the Aces.

The stock is dealt one card at a time and any card that cannot be played to a foundation is played to one of the 20

Foundations

Layout (waste heaps)

cards in the layout, which, in reality, function as waste heaps. The top cards of the waste heaps are available to be played to the foundations, and, when all the cards of a waste heap have been played, the vacancy is filled with a card from the stock.

A card must not be played from one waste heap to another, and no card may be dealt from the stock until the previous one has been placed.

In the example in the illustration, three foundation cards appeared in the initial deal. The ♠A, ♣A and ♦K have been played to the foundation row; the other ♦K may not be used as a foundation card. The ♠2 may be built on the ♠A and the ♠3 on the ♠2.

Congress

HOW TO PLAY

Eight cards are dealt face up to the board in two columns of four cards (see illustration 1).

The object of the game is to play the eight Aces – as they become available – to the centre and build on them ascending suit sequences to the Kings.

The cards in the layout are packed in descending sequences regardless of suit and colour. Only one card may be moved at a time, the stock is turned one card at a time, and a card that cannot be packed on the layout or built on a foundation is played to the waste heap, the top card of which is available to be played. A vacancy in the layout must be filled at once either from the stock or the waste heap; it is permitted to look at the next card from the stock before deciding whether to fill a vacancy with it or the top card of the waste heap. With the cards as dealt in illustration 1, the ♦ A is played to the centre and since, as yet, there is no waste heap the vacancy is filled from the stock. The ♦ 5 is packed on the ♠ 6 and the vacancy filled from the stock.

Illustration 2 shows the same game a little advanced. The ♦ Q is now packed on the ♥ K and the player may look at the next card of the stock and decide whether to fill the vacancy with it or with the ♣ 5.

Illustration 1

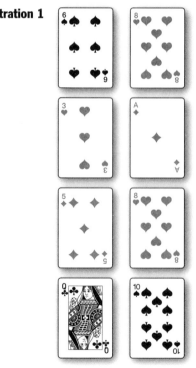

Illustration 2

Foundations

Layout

Waste heap

Corner stones

HOW TO PLAY

The layout of Corner Stones, or Four Corners, is very simple. First, 12 cards are dealt face up to the board in two columns of six cards, with enough room between them to allow for two columns of foundation cards. The top and bottom cards of the two columns are turned horizontally (see illustration).

An Ace and a King of each suit are played to two columns in the centre as they become available, the Ace and King of the same suit being placed side by side. The object of the game is to build on the Aces ascending suit sequences to the Kings, and descending suit sequences to the Aces on the Kings.

The stock is turned one card at a time to cover in turn the cards in the two outer columns, starting at the top of the right-hand column and finishing at the bottom of the left-hand column. While the stock is being dealt, any cards that could be played to a foundation are subject to the following rules:

If a card falls on one of the horizontal cards it may be played to any foundation, but if it would fall on a card in the vertical columns it may be played only to a foundation in the same row.

The horizontal cards and those in the columns must not be deprived of cards, and when a card is played to a foundation the next card in the stock must be dealt to cover the appropriate card in the layout.

When all of the stock has been dealt, the rules are lifted. The top cards of the 12 piles in the layout are exposed and may be built on any foundation, or packed on other exposed cards in ascending, or descending, round-the-corner sequences, regardless of suit and colour.

When the top cards of two foundations of the same suit are in sequence, one may be reversed on the other, with the exception of the Ace or King foundation cards.

Two redeals are allowed. The cards in the layout are picked up in the same order as they are dealt and redealt without shuffling.

In the illustration, which shows the layout during the deal, the ♥A and ♠K were played to the foundation centre during the deal and their places filled by cards from the stock. The ♠Q and ♥2 cannot be built on the foundations because they were dealt to the wrong rows. The stock will now be dealt onto the 12 cards in the layout, beginning with the ♠5 and ending with the ♠3, cards being moved to foundations as appropriate.

TACTICS

Even though the player has three deals in all, it is not an easy game and to be successful the player must make the most of reversing sequences.

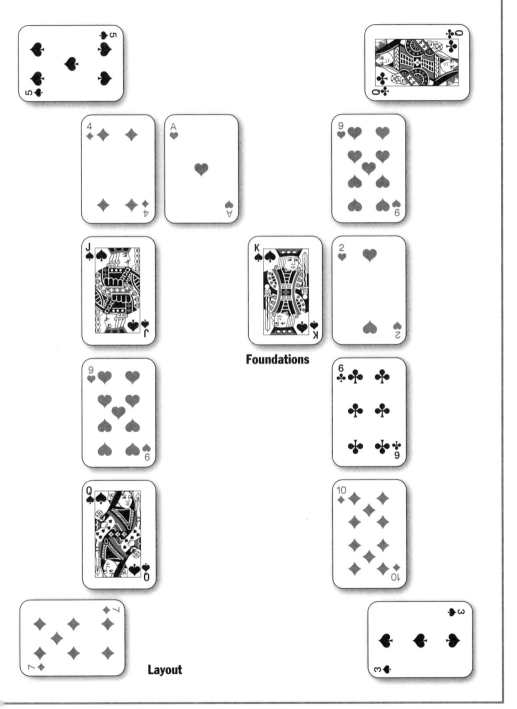

Foundations

Layout

Cromwell

The late Mr Charles Jewell composed a number of double-pack patiences; this is one of his best.

HOW TO PLAY

The whole pack is dealt face up to the board in 26 fans of four cards each. Aces, when they become available, are played to the centre as foundation cards, to be built up to the Kings in ascending suit sequences. The top cards of the fans are exposed: they may be built on the foundations, or packed on other exposed cards in descending suit sequences. A sequence may be moved from one exposed card to another either in part or as a whole, provided that the sequential order is retained. Vacancies in the layout, when all the cards of a fan have been moved, are not filled (see illustration).

Because the vacancies are not filled, the game cannot be won unless at least one King is dealt at the bottom of a fan, so the player has the grace (see Glossary) of being allowed to interchange any two cards once at any stage of the game.

The game shown in the illustration is well advanced, with a reasonable prospect of being won. At this stage, the ♣4 is built on the ♣3, the ♠8 on the ♠7 and the ♦A is played to the foundation row. The ♦2, ♦3, ♦4, ♦5 and ♦6 are built on the ♦A, and the ♣7, ♣8, ♣9, ♣10 and ♣J on the ♣6. The ♥7 and ♥6 are packed on the ♥8, the ♠Q on the ♠K and the ♠J and ♠10 on the ♠Q.

TACTICS

Success depends very largely on looking ahead before making a move. It is essential to take note of the positions occupied by the Kings. The game is likely to be an easy one, and success assured, if two or more Kings are at the bottom of fans.

By contrast, the game will prove a difficult one, calling for consideration before a move is made, if two or three Kings are near the top of their fans. Until those Kings are played (and they can only be played as the last card to a foundation), the lower cards under them are immobilized, and the player must direct his moves towards releasing the duplicates of the immobilized cards. Every effort should be made towards building cards on the foundations, because any card that can be built on a foundation is not pulling its weight if left in the layout.

Foundations

Layout

Diamond

Diamond offers the player little opportunity to exhibit any skill, but it is an interesting game, leisurely, and with an attractive layout.

HOW TO PLAY

First, 41 cards are dealt face up to the board in nine rows, the first and last each of one card, the second and eighth of three cards, the third and seventh of five cards, the fourth and sixth of seven cards and the fifth of nine cards (see illustration).

The object of the game is to play all eight Aces (when they become available) to the centre as foundations, and build on them ascending suit sequences to the Kings.

The cards in the layout are not packed on: they may be used only for building on the foundations, and the player is restricted to moving only those cards with at least one free side (not the top or bottom).

The stock is dealt one card at a time, and any card that cannot be played to a foundation must be played to one of three waste heaps, which are fed in turn from left to right. The top card of a waste heap is available to be played to a foundation, and if two cards are available to be played to the same foundation, the player may play either.

When the stock is exhausted the player fills any vacancies in the layout with the cards that have been played to the left-hand waste heap. If there are not enough cards in that heap to fill all the

vacancies, cards are taken from the middle waste heap, and from the right-hand one if necessary. The player may pick out the cards to fill the vacancies, but must not play any to a foundation.

When the layout has been filled, the cards remaining in the waste heaps are shuffled and dealt.

A third deal is permitted under the same rules. When this deal has been completed, however, if the game has not been won, the cards remaining in the layout and in the waste heaps are shuffled together and a fourth (and final) deal played with a layout of 25 cards; namely a diamond of seven rows, the first and last each of one card, the second and sixth of three cards, the third and fifth of five cards and the fourth of seven cards.

This second diamond should result in the game being successful, but there is no guarantee.

In the layout illustrated, the ♥A is played to the centre and the ♥2 built on it. The ♠A is played to the centre and the ♠2 built on it. The ♣A is played to the centre and the ♣2 built on it. The player has the option of building on the ♠2 either the ♠3 in the third row or that in the seventh row; he will choose the latter because it frees the ♥3 that is built on the ♥2.

Diavolo

HOW TO PLAY

First, 45 cards are dealt face down to the board in nine overlapping rows, the first of nine cards, the second of eight cards, the third of seven cards, down to a row of only one card. Turn the bottom card of each column face up (see illustration).

The object of the game is to release two black Aces and two red Aces, play them to the centre as foundation cards and build on them ascending colour sequences to the Kings and, simultaneously, to pack within the layout descending sequences of alternating colours from the Kings to the Aces.

The face-up cards at the foot of the columns may be built on the foundations, or packed on other exposed cards in the layout in descending sequences of alternating colours. A sequence may be moved either wholly or in part from one exposed card to another, so long as the sequential order and colour alternation is retained. When a complete sequence from King to Ace has been packed in the layout, it may be taken out of the game (but see tactics, below). When a card is moved from the foot of a column, the face-down card immediately above it is turned face up and becomes available for play.

A vacancy in the layout, when all the cards of a column have been played or a complete sequence removed, is filled either with a King or a sequence headed by a King.

The stock is turned one card at a time, and any card that cannot be built on a foundation or packed on the layout is played to a waste heap, the top card of which is always available to be played. The game ends when the stock is exhausted.

With a starting layout as in the illustration, the ♣A is played to the centre and the ♠2 built on it. The ♣Q is packed on the ♥K, the ♦9 on the ♠10 and the ♠4 on the ♦5.

TACTICS

Diavolo is far from an easy game, and success is rare. It is well named. Good judgement is essential because building ascending sequences on the foundations clashes with packing descending sequences on the Kings in the layout. All the time the player has to decide whether a card should be built on an Ace-sequence or packed on a King-sequence, and sometimes it is best to do neither and leave the card where it is, to help towards clearing a column later on.

The comparatively large number of face-down cards in the three columns on the left of the layout usually present difficulties. Every effort should be made to reduce their number, even at the cost of foregoing other plays.

A complete King to Ace sequence within the layout should not be taken out of the game at once. By leaving it in the game it may prove useful to split in order to reach face-down cards in the layout.

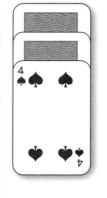

Dieppe

HOW TO PLAY

Remove the Aces from the pack and play them to the centre as foundation cards, which will have ascending suit sequences to the Kings built on them.

Below the Aces, deal a row of eight cards face up to the board, playing any available ones to a foundation and filling the vacancies with cards from the stock. When the row is complete, and no further cards can be built on foundations, deal a second row in the same manner, and after that a third. For convenience the cards in the rows may overlap (see illustration).

The cards in the bottom row of the layout are exposed and may be built on a foundation, or packed on other exposed cards in descending sequences irrespective of suit and colour. A sequence may be moved either in whole

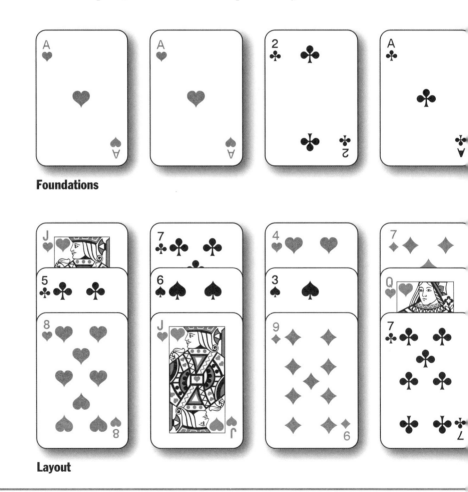

Foundations

Layout

or in part from one exposed card to another, so long as the sequential order is retained. If all the cards of a column are moved, the vacancy may be filled by any exposed card or sequence of cards.

The stock is dealt one card at a time and any card that cannot be built on a foundation or packed on the layout is played to a waste heap, the top card of which is always available. There is no second deal.

In the illustration, the ♣2 and ♦2 and ♦3 were played to the foundation row during the deal. The ♥J is packed on the ♣Q, the ♥8 on the ♦9, the ♣7 on the ♥8, the ♥5 on the ♠6, the ♠10 on the ♥J and the ♠4 on the ♥5. The vacancy is filled by the ♣Q with the ♥J and ♠10. Once no more moves can be played with the cards in the layout, cards can be played from the stock.

Diplomat

HOW TO PLAY

Eight fans of four cards are dealt face up to the board (see illustration). The eight Aces are played to a foundation row as they become available, to be built on in ascending suit sequences to the Kings.

The exposed top cards of the fans are available to be built on the foundations, or packed on other exposed cards in the layout in descending sequences regardless of suit and colour. Sequences and part-sequences may be moved from one fan to another, provided the sequential order is retained. A vacancy made by clearing a fan may be filled by any available card.

The stock is dealt one card at a time, and any card that cannot be played to a foundation or to the layout is played to the waste heap, the top card of which is available.

With the initial layout in the illustration, the ♠8 is packed on the ♦9 and the ♥10 on the ♠J. The ♦7 is packed on the ♠8 and the ♥6 on the ♦7. The ♣2 is packed on the ♠3, the vacancy filled by the ♣4 and the ♥A is played to the foundation row. The ♠J with the ♥10 is packed on the ♥Q, and the ♣A is played to the foundation row. When all possible moves within the layout have been exhausted, cards can be played from the stock.

Display

This is an interesting and a unique game that calls for more watchfulness than skill.

HOW TO PLAY

The top card of the pack is dealt face up to the left of the board and further cards dealt one at a time. The object of the game is to arrange the whole pack in round-the-corner sequences, regardless of suit and colour, in eight rows. In the illustration, the eight rows are in place. Any card that cannot be played to the layout is played to one of three waste heaps, at the player's discretion. Suppose that the first card dealt is the ♥9. When the 10 of any suit is dealt it is played to the right of the 9, and when the Jack of any suit is dealt it is played to the right of the 10. An 8 is played below the 9, and a 7 below the 8. The illustration shows how such a game may develop.

No card may be played to the layout unless the previous one is in position, but the top cards of the waste heaps are always available to be played.

When the pack is exhausted the waste heaps are gathered and redealt, this time with only one waste heap. There is no third deal.

TACTICS

It helps towards success to keep the eight rows as nearly as possible to the same length, and not to play too many cards of one rank to the same waste heap.

Layout

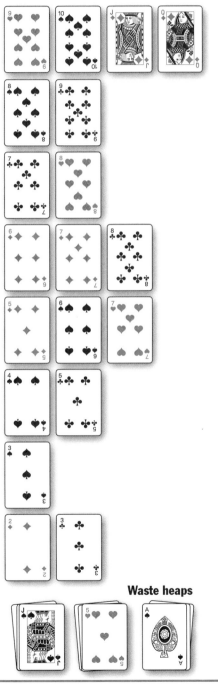

Waste heaps

Dog

HOW TO PLAY

An Ace and a King of each suit are removed from the pack and played to the centre as foundation cards. The Aces are built on in ascending suit sequences to the Kings, the Kings in descending suit sequences to the Aces.

The rest of the pack is dealt face up to the board in 13 piles. As the cards are dealt, the player calls 'Ace' as a card is played to the first pile, 'Two' for the second, and so on to 'King' for the thirteenth. Whenever the card dealt matches the call it is not played to the pile, but put aside face down to a heel,

and the next card of the pack dealt to the pile in its place (see illustration).

The top cards of the piles are exposed and, when the whole pack has been dealt, but not before, are available to be built on the foundations. When a card is taken off a pile the one immediately under it becomes available for play.

When all plays have been made, the top card of the heel is taken up and is available to be built on a foundation; if it cannot be played immediately the pile whose number corresponds to that of the card is taken in hand and sorted. Cards that can be built on the foundations should be played; the remaining cards

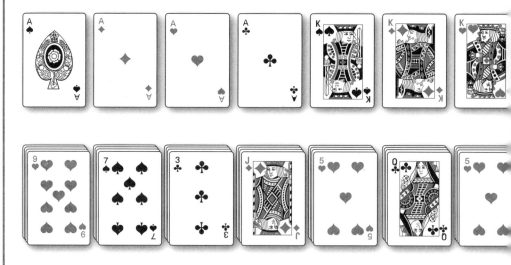

may be arranged in any order that the player chooses (the top card should be the one most likely to become playable to a foundation as the succeeding piles are sorted). The pile is replaced on the board, but turned at 90 degrees to show that it has been sorted, because each pile may be sorted only once. If a second card of the same rank is drawn from the heel, the player may lift and sort any pile that has not already been picked up.

Each card in the heel is treated in the same way, and if any cards are left in the heel after all the piles have been sorted, they are turned face up and become available to be built on the foundations.

Two redeals are allowed. Piles one to six are picked up in this order, pile 13 and any cards left in the heel are placed on top of them, and piles 12 to seven are picked up in this order and placed on top of the pack. The redeals are dealt and played in the same way as the first deal.

At any time during the play any card that is in sequence and of the same suit may be moved from an Ace foundation to a King foundation or vice versa.

With a starting layout as shown in the illustration, the ♣2 is built on the ♣A, the ♣3 on the ♣2 and the ♦2 on the ♦A. The ♣Q is built on the ♣K and the ♥Q on the ♥K. And so on.

Foundations

Heel

Eight by eight

Eight by eight is a simple, but nonetheless interesting, building-up patience.

HOW TO PLAY

First, 64 cards are dealt face up to the board in eight overlapping rows of eight cards (see illustration).

The object of the game is to release the eight Aces, play them to the centre as foundation cards, and build on them ascending suit sequences to the Kings.

The bottom card of a column is exposed. It may be built on a foundation, or packed on another exposed card in a descending sequence regardless of suit and colour. A sequence may be moved from one column to another either as a whole or in part, but a vacancy, when all the cards of a column have been moved,

may be filled only by a single, exposed card, or by a suit sequence where all the cards are of the same suit.

The stock is dealt in bundles of three cards to the waste heap; if at the end of the stock there are fewer than three cards, they are dealt singly. If a redeal is necessary the waste heap is picked up and dealt two cards at a time, and if a further redeal is necessary, the cards are dealt singly. No more than two redeals are allowed. The top card of the waste heap is always available to be played.

In the illustration, the ♦9 is packed on the ♠10, then the ♠10 and ♦9 on the ♥J and the ♥8 on the ♦9. The ♣4 is packed on the ♦5, the ♥A is played to the centre and the ♥2 built on the ♥A. The ♦5 with the ♣4 is packed on the ♠6 and the three of them on the ♣7. The ♠A is played to the centre.

The Emperor

The Emperor is a patience that lends itself to forethought and much ingenuity.

HOW TO PLAY

First, 30 cards are dealt to the board face down in ten packs of three cards; these are known as the sealed packets. Ten more cards are dealt face up in a row below the packets. Aces, as they occur, are played to the centre as foundation cards, to be built on in ascending suit sequences to the Kings (see illustration).

The ten cards below the sealed packets are available to be packed with cards dealt from the stock, and may be packed on each other in descending sequences of alternating colours. Sequences and part-sequences may be moved from one column to another, provided the sequential order and alternation of colour are retained. Worrying back (see Glossary) is allowed.

When all the cards of a column have been played, the top card of the sealed packet immediately above the vacancy is turned face up and brought into play. It need not necessarily be used to fill the vacancy, which may be filled by any exposed card or a sequence.

The stock is dealt one card at a time, and any card that cannot be built on a foundation or packed on the layout is played to the waste heap, the top card of which is available to be played.

When the stock is exhausted, the waste heap is taken in hand as a new stock. The three top cards are dealt face

up on the table as a reserve. If any or all of them can be played, cards from the stock are dealt to bring the reserve up to three cards. Play continues in this way until the game either succeeds, or fails

because the stock is exhausted a second time and none of the cards in the reserve can be played.

In the illustration, which shows a game in progress, the ♥4 from the waste heap is packed on the ♠5, the ♠3 from the foundation on the ♥4, the ♦2 on the ♠3 and the top card of the sealed packet above the ♦2 brought into play. The ♦7 is packed on the ♠8 and the top card of the sealed packet above the ♦7 brought into play. The ♠6 and the ♦5 are packed on the ♦7 and the top card of the sealed packet above the ♠6 brought into play.

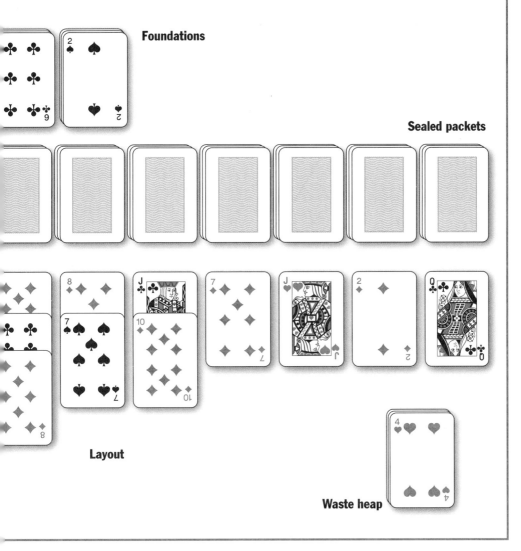

Foundations

Sealed packets

Layout

Waste heap

Fandango

HOW TO PLAY

First, 60 cards are played to the board face up in 20 fans of three cards each. If any Aces occur in the fans they are played to the centre as foundation cards and replaced in the fans with cards from the stock. As they become available, the other Aces are played to the centre (see illustration). The object of the game is to build on the Aces ascending suit sequences to the Kings.

The exposed cards of the fans are available to be built on the foundations, or they may be packed on each other in ascending or descending suit sequences that may be reversed at will. Single cards only are moved, but since sequences can be ascending or descending, whole or part of a sequence can be moved card by card. A vacancy in the layout, caused by all the cards of a fan being played, is filled by a new fan of three cards from the stock. The stock is not turned but used only to replace any of the fans.

Three deals are allowed. When no further moves can be made, the layout is picked up, shuffled with any cards left in the stock, and redealt to the board in 20 fans of three cards each, or as many fans as the cards allow. If it is fewer than 20, and one or two cards are left over, the odd cards form a small fan of their own.

In the layout illustrated, the ♥4 is¹ packed on the ♥5, the ♠7 on the ♠8, the ♠6 on the ♠7 and the ♦9 on the ♦10. The ♥K is packed on the ♥Q and the ♥Q on the ♥K. And so on.

Four square

Four Square is considered an easy game that the player will win every time unless playing carelessly or dogged by bad luck.

HOW TO PLAY

An Ace and a King of each suit are removed from the pack and played to the board as foundation cards. The remainder of the pack is dealt face down in 16 piles of six cards, arranged in a square with the foundation cards in the middle, and with the top card of each pile turned face up (see illustration).

The object of the game is to build on the Aces ascending suit sequences to the Kings, and descending suit sequences to the Aces on the Kings. When the top cards of two foundations of the same suit are in sequence, the cards of either, except the original Ace or King foundation card, may be reversed onto the other (see Glossary).

The top cards of the piles are exposed and may be built on the foundations, or packed on each other either in ascending or descending suit sequences, which may be on the same pile. Only one card may be moved at a time, and when a card is taken from a pile the card under it is turned face up and becomes available for play. A vacancy, when all the cards of a pile have been played, is not filled. When all possible moves have been made and play comes to a standstill, the player has the grace (see Glossary) of bringing the bottom cards of some or all of the piles to the top. Three such graces are allowed.

With the layout in the illustration, the ♥2 is built on the ♥A and the ♥Q on the ♥K. The ♠3 is packed on the ♠4 (or vice versa) and the ♦10 on the ♦J (or vice versa).

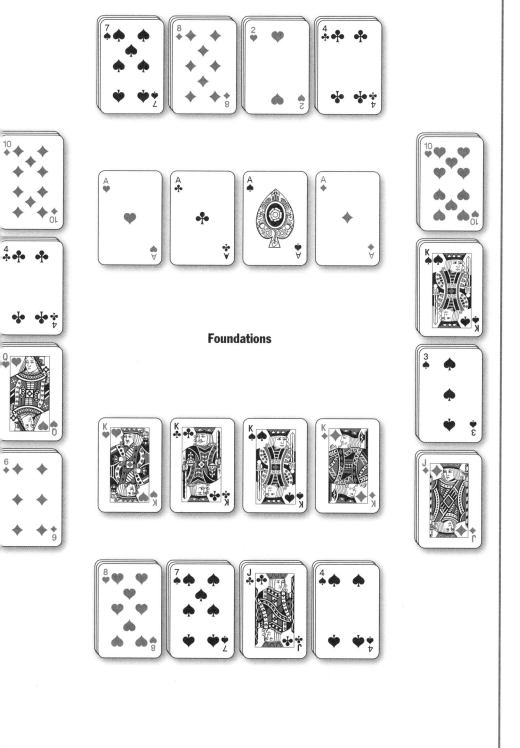

Foundations

Fourteens

Fourteens is one of several two-pack patience games composed by Mr Charles Jewell.

HOW TO PLAY

First, 48 cards are dealt in the form of an open cross (see illustration). To win the game the table must be cleared of every card in the pack. Counting the Jacks as 11, the Queens as 12 and the Kings as 13, any two adjacent cards, touching at the sides, the corners or at top and bottom are discarded if together they have a pip total of fourteen. There is, however, no compulsion to discard a touching pair. When two cards have been discarded, those that remain on the table are closed up towards the centre of the cross, but not from one quarter into another. When all the discards have been made, and the cards that remain on the table have been closed up, the layout is filled with cards from the stock.

In the layout illustrated, the ♥J and ♠3 in the fourth quarter are discarded and the ♠5 and ♦8 moved to the left. Now the ♦Q may be moved either up or to the left and very clearly it should be moved to the left so that it may be paired and discarded with the ♦2. The ♣4 and ♠9 are moved up, the ♠K and ♥A are discarded, and the ♠6 is moved up. In the second quarter the ♠3 and ♦J are discarded, and the ♣6 and ♠K moved down. This allows the ♣6 (in the second

quarter) to be paired and discarded with the ♦8 (in the fourth quarter) and the ♠K (in the second quarter) to be moved to the left. The layout is very favourable to success, because in the first quarter the ♠J may be discarded with the ♥3, the ♥6 and ♣3 moved to the right, and the ♥8 and ♠6 discarded. In the second quarter the ♠J and ♣3 may be discarded and the ♦7 moved down. In the third quarter there is the choice of discarding the ♦3 with the ♦J or with the ♣J.

TACTICS

The game calls for considerable foresight, and a watchful eye must be kept on the four cards at the centre of the cross, because unless they can be paired and discarded the movement of the layout towards the centre is obstructed. Very often it is unwise to discard a pair and better to keep it in reserve. Judicious pairing and discarding, coupled with skilful movements in closing up, help in getting the right card into position to get rid of a card that is holding up the game at the centre of the cross. The endgame calls for exact play, because it usually contains a number of traps into which it is very easy for the thoughtless player to fall.

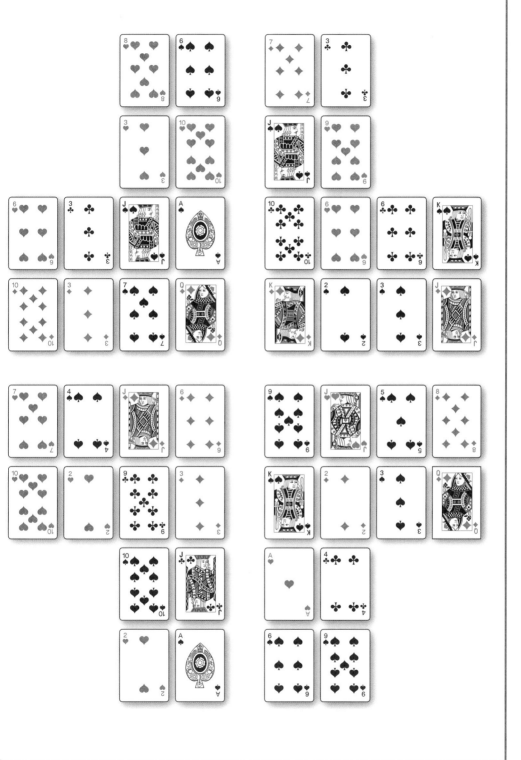

Half moon

HOW TO PLAY

Eight cards are dealt to the board face up in a row as a reserve. The rest of the pack is then dealt face down in 12 packets of eight cards. The packets should be arranged in a semi-circle above the reserve, and the top card of each packet turned face up (see illustration).

The object of the game is to discard the pack by taking out of the game any two exposed cards with pips that total 11, and any sequences of Jack, Queen and King, irrespective of suit, which are exposed together.

When the top card of a packet is taken, the card under it is turned face up and becomes available for play. A card must not be taken from the reserve if one of the same rank can be taken from a packet; and if two or more cards of the same rank are available on top of the packets, the cards under them may be examined to determine which one is the best to take.

With the layout illustrated, the ♠6 is taken with the ♥5. The cards under the ♥3 and ♦3 are checked in order to determine which is the better to take with the ♥8, as are the cards under the ♣7 and ♠7 to see which is the better to take with the ♠4. The ♥9 is taken either with the ♠2 or ♣2, and the ♦10 with the ♠A.

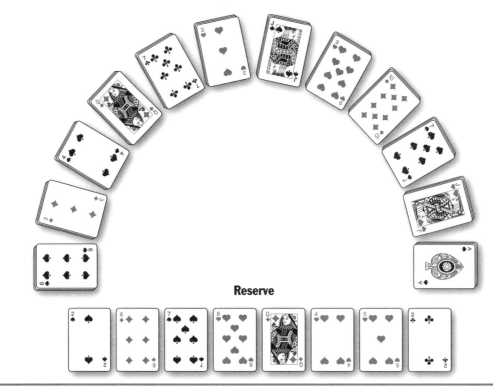

Reserve

Heads and tails

HOW TO PLAY

A row of eight cards (the heads) is dealt face up to the board, then a row of eight packets of 11 cards, then a further row of eight cards (the tails) (see illustration).

The object of the game is to release one Ace and one King of each suit, play them to the centre as foundation cards, and build on the Aces ascending suit sequences to the Kings and descending suit sequences to the Aces on the Kings.

Only the cards in the top and bottom rows are available to be built on the foundations. They may also be packed in ascending and descending, round-the-corner suit sequences, which may be changed at will. The cards from the middle row of packets are used only to fill vacancies in the top and bottom rows. The card must be taken from the packet immediately above or below the vacancy, unless the packet has already been emptied, in which case a card may be taken from any packet.

With a layout as illustrated, the ♠A is played to the centre and the ♥9 fills the vacancy. The ♦K is played to the centre, the ♦Q is built on it and the ♣8 and ♣4 fill the vacancies. The ♠J is packed on the ♠Q, the ♠10 on the ♠J, and the vacancies filled by the ♣10 and ♥7.

Heads

Tails

Heap

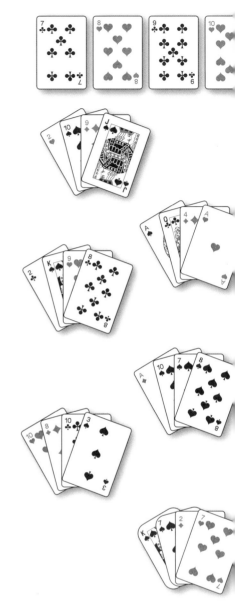

HOW TO PLAY

A sequence of 13 cards, from a 7 to a 6 in alternating colours is laid out as foundation cards. The suits are immaterial. The rest of the pack is dealt face up to the board in 22 fans of four cards and one of three cards (see illustration).

The object of the game is to build on the 13 foundation cards numeral-sequences of eight cards in the same colour on the first 12, and in alternating colours on the thirteenth. If the game is successful (and it should be with the exercise of forethought) it will show a sequence from Ace to Jack in alternating colours and the Queen and King of the same colour.

Packing is not allowed on the layout, and vacancies created by all the cards of a fan being played are not filled. The top cards of the fans are available to be built on the foundations and, when every available card has been built on the foundations, those remaining in the layout are picked up, shuffled and redealt in fans of four each. If one, two or three cards are left over, they have a fan to themselves. Only two deals are allowed.

In the illustration, the ♦J is built on the ♥10, the ♦2 on the ♥A, the ♣10 on the ♣9, the ♠J on the ♣10, the ♦7 on the ♣6 and the ♠8 on the ♦7. And so on. The sequences on the foundation cards should be kept as equal as possible.

TACTICS

Nothing is to be gained by playing off all the cards of a fan, because the vacancy is not filled, so if two cards of the same rank are available at the same time, the one from the fan with more cards in it should be played.

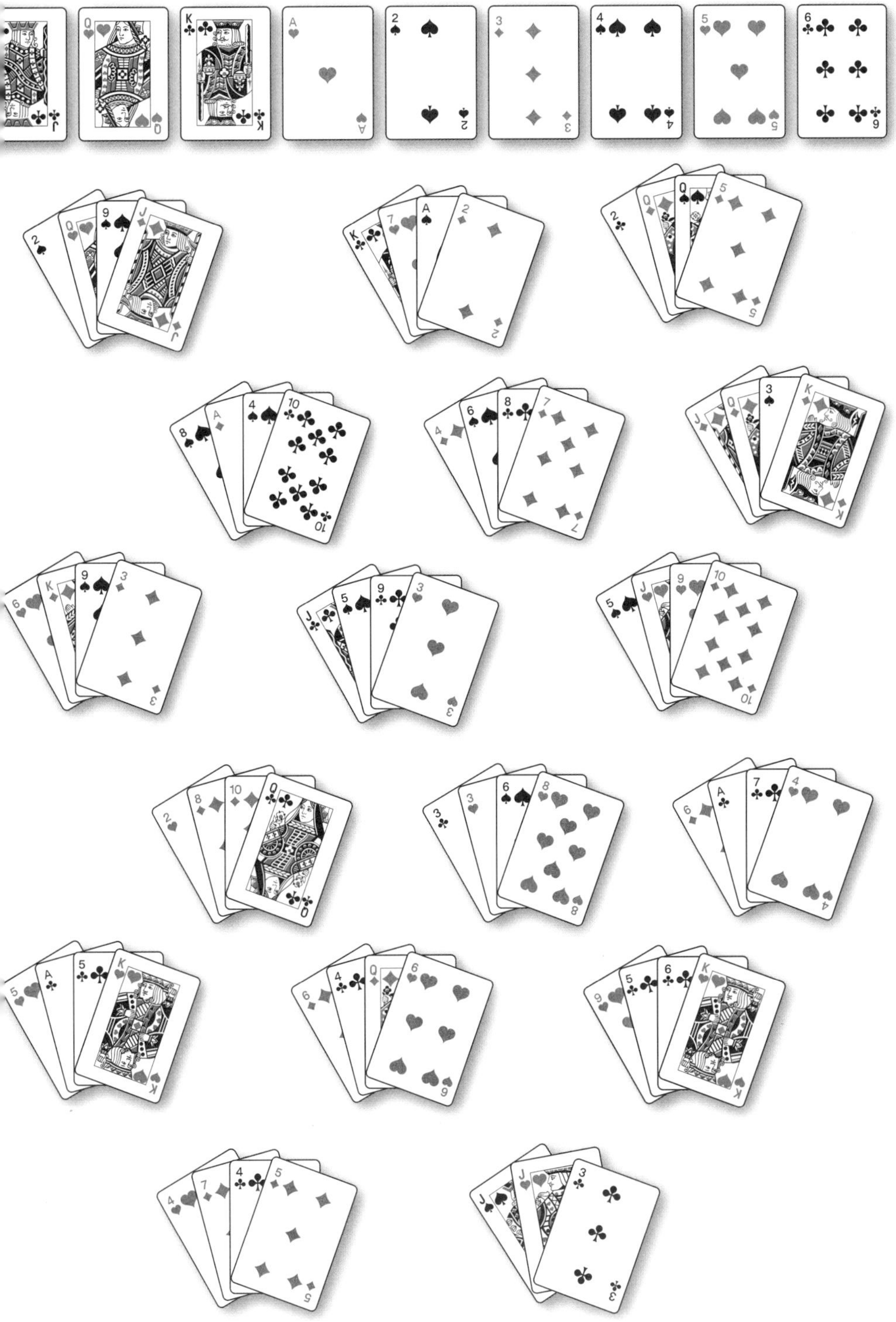

Indian carpet

Indian Carpet, Crazy Quilt, Japanese Rug or Quilt, is a two-pack patience with a very attractive layout.

Layout

HOW TO PLAY

An Ace and a King of each suit are played to the centre as foundations. Below them, 64 cards are dealt face up in eight rows of eight cards, laid vertically and horizontally in turn (see illustration).

The Ace foundations are built on in ascending suit sequences to the Kings, and the King foundations in descending suit sequences to the Aces.

Any card in the layout is available for play, provided that one of its shorter sides is not touching another card. Thus in the layout illustrated, the ♠2 in the top row may be built on its Ace foundation, but the ♥2 may not. The play of the ♠2 leaves the ♦5 and ♠J free to be played later.

Spaces in the layout are not filled, and the cards in the layout are not packed. The remaining 32 cards in the stock are turned one at a time, and any card that cannot be built on a foundation is played to the waste heap. The top card of the waste heap is always available to be built on the foundations. Available cards in the layout may be packed on the top card of the waste heap in either ascending or descending round-the-corner suit sequences.

The waste heap may be redealt once.

Kings' way

Kings' way is unlike any other game of patience. For this reason, and no other, it is included in this collection. Except for originality it is a game with few merits but amusement and it gives no scope for skill or ingenuity. Success depends entirely on the lucky order of the cards.

HOW TO PLAY

The eight Kings are removed from the pack and played in a row face up to the top of the board. Below them 40 cards are dealt in five overlapping rows of eight cards, the first four rows face down, the fifth face up (see illustration).

The object of the game is to clear the 40 cards (not including the Kings) dealt to the board, so that the road is open to the Kings – the Kings' way.

There is no building on foundations and no packing on cards in the layout. The stock is dealt one card at a time to a waste heap and the eight cards in the bottom row of the layout are exposed and may be packed on the top card of the waste heap in either ascending or descending sequence of alternating

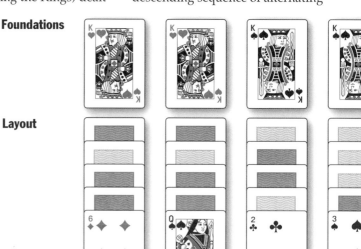

Foundations

Layout

colours. When a card from the bottom row of the layout is packed on the waste heap, the card in the row above it is turned face up and becomes available.

Aces are given special treatment. If one is turned up in the layout it can only be moved when a 2 of the other colour is the top card of the waste heap. If one is dealt from the stock to the waste heap it may be packed with a 2 of the other colour if one is exposed in the layout, as also may subsequent cards in sequence, i.e if there a a red 2 in the layout, a black Ace may be packed with it, followed by a black 3, etc. If no 2 of alternating colour is exposed in the layout, the Ace is moved to a separate waste heap, as are any others that are dealt when no 2 is available. They remain there until the stock is exhausted and, if the game has not already been won, the number of Aces in the waste heap determines the number of cards that may be taken from the beginning of the waste heap and dealt a second time.

From the layout illustrated the ♠9 is packed on the ♦10 and the player has the option of packing either the ♥10 or the ♥8 on the ♠9. It would be best to choose the ♥8, because if a black 7 is turned up, it can then be packed on the ♥8 and followed by the ♦6.

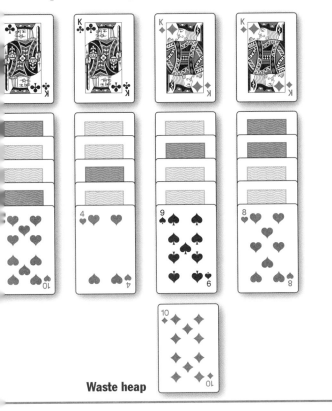

Waste heap

123

Lady Palk

Whoever Lady Palk was or is, she has certainly given her name to an interesting patience.

HOW TO PLAY

First, 16 cards are dealt face up to the board in four columns of four cards. This is the left wing. Then another, similar, group of 16 cards is dealt to the right (the right wing), leaving a space wide enough to accommodate the Aces in two columns of four cards.

The object of the game is to release the Aces, play them to the centre as foundation cards, and build on them ascending suit sequences to the Kings.

The cards in the left-hand column of the left wing, and the right-hand column of the right wing, are available for play. When one has been played, the next card becomes the outside card. Cards are not

Left wing

replaced until a whole row on either the left or right wing becomes vacant, when it may be filled by a King. If a King cannot played, it stays vacant until a King becomes available. Exposed cards may be built on the foundations or packed on each other in descending sequences irrespective of suit and colour. Single cards and part or whole sequences may be moved from an exposed card to any other, provided the sequential order is retained.

The stock is dealt one card at a time. Any card that cannot be built on a foundation or packed on the layout is played to the waste heap, the top card of which is available for play. The stock is dealt only once, but worrying back (see Glossary) is allowed during the game.

In the layout illustrated, the ♦3 is packed on the ♠4 and the ♣2 on the ♦3. The ♠8 is packed on the ♦9, the ♠7 on the ♠8, the ♥6 on the ♠7 and the ♠5 on the ♥6. The ♣2 from the right wing is packed on the ♣3, the ♣A is played to the centre, and the ♣2 and ♣3 built on the ♣A.

Right wing

Le cadran

Le cadran is described by Lady Adelaide Cadogan in her Illustrated Games
of Patience *of c.1870. It is, therefore, one of the oldest, if not the oldest, of
the many building-up patience games.*

HOW TO PLAY

First, 40 cards are dealt face up to the
board in four overlapping rows of ten
cards (see illustration).

The object of the game is to release
the eight Aces, play them to the centre as
foundation cards, and build on them
ascending suit sequences to the Kings.

The bottom cards of the columns are
available to be played to the foundations,
or packed on each other in descending
suit sequences. Cards must be moved
only singly, not in sequences.

A vacancy, when all the cards of a
column have been played, is filled either

with an exposed card from the layout or
with the top card of the waste heap.

The stock is dealt one card at a time
and any card that cannot be built on a
foundation or packed on the layout is
played to the waste heap, the top card of
which is always available. There is no
second deal.

With the deal illustrated, play the
♠A to the centre, build the ♠2 on the
♠A and the ♠3 on the ♠2. Play the ♥A
to the centre. Pack the ♦10 on the ♦J,
the ♠9 on the ♠10, the ♦9 on the ♦10,
the ♦8 on the ♦9, the ♦7 on the ♦8 and
the ♦6 on the ♦7.

Le chateau

HOW TO PLAY

First, 60 cards are dealt face up to the board in 12 packets of five cards, in a row of three packets, then of four packets and of five packets, touching each other only at the corners (see illustration).

The object of the game is to release the Aces, play them to the centre as foundation cards and build them up in suit sequences to the Kings.

The top cards of the packet are exposed and may be built on a foundation, or packed on each other in a descending sequence of alternating colours. A sequence may be moved from one packet or another either as a whole

or in part, so long as the sequence and alternation of colour are retained.

The stock is turned one card at a time, and any card that cannot be played to a foundation or to a packet is played to a waste heap, the top card of which is always available for play.

A vacancy, caused by all the cards of a packet having been played, may be filled with the top card of the waste heap, or by a card, sequence or part-sequence from one of the packets.

In the layout shown, the ♠A is played to the centre, and ♥2 is packed on the ♠3, the ♣9 on the ♥10 and the ♥6 on the ♣7.

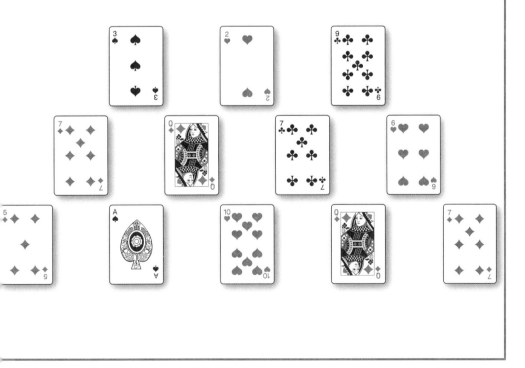

Limited

Limited is an improvement on a game called Napoleon at St Helena, which is not the game called St Helena described elsewhere in this book. It is unlikely that Napoleon played either game.

HOW TO PLAY

Three rows of 12 cards are laid out face up. Any Aces in the bottom row are played to the centre as a foundation, as are Aces turned up from stock during the play. Any Aces in the first two rows of the layout must stay there until they become exposed by the lower cards being played elsewhere. Only the lowest card in a column is available for play. The object of the game is to build on the Aces ascending suit sequences to the Kings.

The game gets its name by the limited amount of packing possible. A card can be packed from one column onto an exposed card in another column in downward suit sequence (such as ♦4 on ♦5), but the couple thus made cannot be further packed upon or moved to another column. They can only be moved when played to a foundation as a pair. Packed cards should overlap, thus distinguishing them as a couple.

If any columns become vacant, they can be filled by any available cards, i.e. the bottom card of any other column (unless it is one of a couple) or the top card of the waste heap. Vacancies need not be filled immediately.

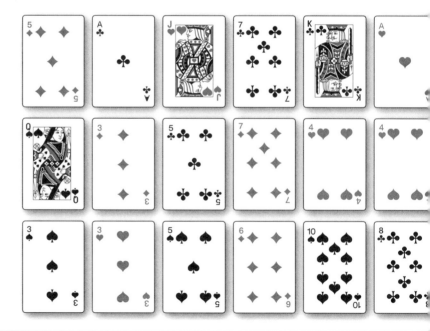

The stock is turned one card at a time, and either played to a foundation or packed on an available card (making a couple). Packing is not obligatory, and indeed it is sometimes best avoided. When the stock is exhausted,the player is allowed a limited second turn. The waste pile is turned over and the first four cards dealt in a line face up. These are known as 'grace cards', and are available to be played to a foundation, a vacancy or packed on a column, which may allow other plays. Further cards are dealt to fill the grace card row to four, and play is continued. When none of the grace cards fits, the player may look at a fifth card, if that cannot be played the game is over.

The description of this patience makes it appear impossible to win, and it seems more so when the waste heap grows alarmingly as it usually does in the early stages. But even if the waste heap when turned over contains 30–40 cards, it is still possible for the game to be won.

In the deal illustrated, the ♦ A and ♠ A should be played to the foundations, followed by the ♠2, ♠3, ♠4 and ♠5. The ♠Q is packed on the ♠K and then the player can start to turn over the stock.

TACTICS

It is not always good policy to pack cards, especially if it means that low cards in the top two rows will become blocked. Vacancies are very useful, especially when the grace cards come into operation, and should not be filled too hastily.

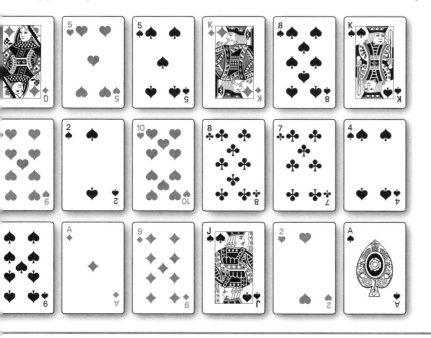

Matrimony

This is rather a difficult game but it has the merit of an unusual layout and play.

HOW TO PLAY

One ◆Q and ◆J are removed from the pack and played to the centre as foundation cards. As they become available, the two ♥Js and the four black 10s are also played to the centre. Below the foundation row, 16 cards are dealt, face up, in two rows of eight cards (see illustration); foundation cards are played directly to the centre.

The object of the game is to build an ascending suit sequence on the ◆Q to the ◆J, and descending suit sequences on the three Jacks to the Queens, and on the four 10s to the Jacks. In all cases, of course, the sequences are round-the-corner, an Ace being above the King and below the 2.

The cards in the layout are exposed and available to be built on the foundations. When all plays have been

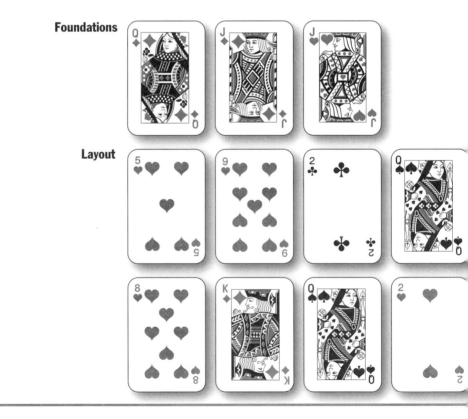

Foundations

Layout

made, 16 cards are dealt from the stock to the layout, covering the cards that have not been played from it and filling the vacancies left by those that have. Play is continued in this way until the stock is exhausted.

When play comes to a standstill and the stock is exhausted, each pile in turn (beginning with the one at the extreme right of the lower row) is picked up and dealt from left to right as far as it will go, the first card being dealt to the vacancy made where the pile was taken up. Once the moves have been exhausted with the redealt cards then the next pile (the

second from the right of the lower row) is picked up and dealt in the same way, and so on. The game ends, if it has not been won before, after the pile at the extreme left of the upper row has been dealt.

In the illustration, the ♥J and ♠10 were played to the foundation row during the deal. The ♦K is built on the ♦Q and the ♠9 on the ♠10. No further plays are available, so 16 cards are dealt from the stock covering the unplayed cards and filling the two vacancies.

Miss Milligan

This is a classic patience game, the enduring popularity of which must be due, in part, to its amazing ability to turn out from apparently hopeless positions.

HOW TO PLAY

Eight cards from two packs shuffled together are dealt side by side, face up. Any Aces are taken out and played to the centre as foundation cards – the object of the game is to build ascending suit sequences up to the Kings on them. The remaining cards are built on the Aces, or packed on each other in descending sequences of alternating colours. Only the Kings may be moved into vacancies.

When no further building or packing can be done, another eight cards are dealt on the piles (or into vacancies), then built and packed again. Any card or properly packed sequence may be moved from one pile and packed onto another pile, providing the sequential order and alternating colours are maintained. Aces are taken out as they appear, and building onto them is allowed during packing.

The illustration shows a position reached after three deals and some

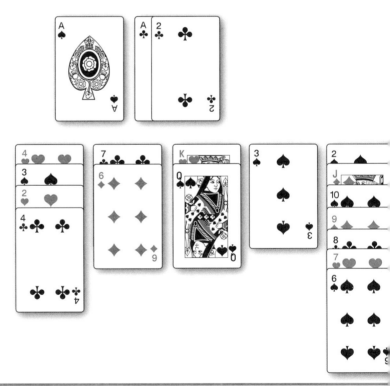

packing. From this position the sequence from ♦J down to ♠6 may be packed onto the ♠Q, then the ♠2 built onto the ♠A, and the ♠3 onto the ♠2. No more packing can be done, so eight more cards are then dealt.

Alternate phases of packing and dealing are continued until the stock has been exhausted. The position may look hopeless, with all the vital cards buried, but at this point a new manoeuvre is allowed – waiving. This simply means to pick up the top card from one of the piles and retain it in the hand, allowing play to continue until it can be built or packed. Only one card may be waived at a time, but this should suffice to bring the patience out. Some people allow a whole sequence to be waived at once so long as it is properly packed.

TACTICS

A technique which is particularly useful in Miss Milligan is the transfer of parts of sequences. If, for instance, an awkward sequence with a black Jack at the top is blocking one of the piles and another black Jack is exposed elsewhere, the bottom part of the sequence from the red 10 down may be transferred to the other Jack, then the first Jack waived, allowing the rest of the pile to be built and packed as required.

Mount Olympus

HOW TO PLAY

Remove the Aces and 2s from the pack and play them to the centre in two rows (the Aces above the 2s) as foundation cards. Below them, deal a row of nine cards face up (see illustration).

The object of the game is to build suit sequences on the Aces in the order

A, 3, 5, 7, 9, J, K and on the 2s in the order 2, 4, 6, 8, 10, Q.

The cards in the layout are available to be built on the foundations, or packed on each other in descending suit sequences by twos. A sequence may be moved only as a whole, and a vacancy, caused by moving a card or sequence, must be filled from the stock.

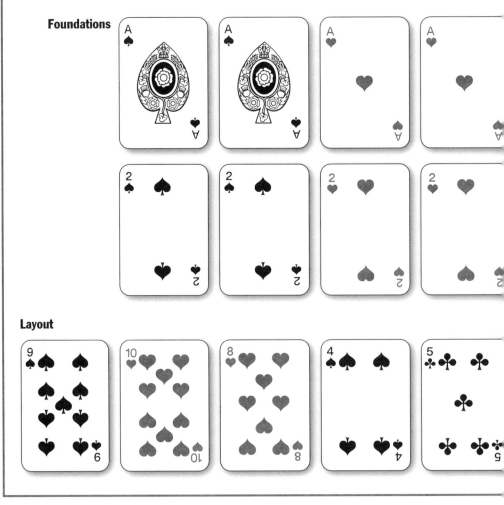

Foundations

Layout

When play comes to a standstill, all vacancies must be filled and, if no further moves can be made, a row of nine cards is dealt on top of those in the layout. The top cards of the piles in the layout are exposed and available for play.

In the layout illustrated, the ♥8 is packed on the ♥10. The ♣3 is built on an ♣A and the ♣5 on the ♣3. The

vacancies are filled by cards from the stock and, if none can be built on the foundations or packed on exposed cards in the layout, a row of cards is dealt on top of those in the layout and play continues as before.

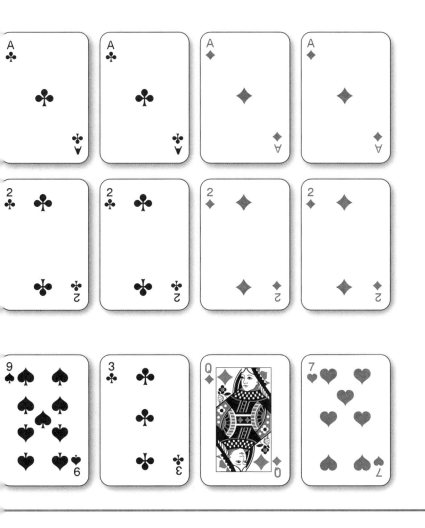

Mrs Mop

Mrs Mop, a patience invented by the late Mr Charles Jewell, is rather a deceptive game. It appears to be easy, but, in fact, is not. Success comes only if thought is given to every move, sometimes right up to the end of the game. The name is an appropriate one, because if the player is to succeed he must clear, or mop up, a column early in the game, in order to gain a vacancy to transfer cards from one column to another. Without one the chance of success is remote.

HOW TO PLAY

The whole pack is dealt face up to the board in eight overlapping rows of 13 cards (see illustration).

The object of the game is to build within the layout eight descending suit sequences to the Aces on the Kings.

The cards at the foot of the columns may be packed on each other in

descending sequences regardless of suit and colour. Only one card may be moved at a time, unless two or more cards are in suit sequence, in which case they must all be moved together.

When all the cards of a column have been moved, the vacancy may be filled by either a single card or a suit sequence of cards.

Beginning with the layout as illustrated, the ♣J is packed on the ♣Q, the ♠9 on the ♠10, the ♣2 on the ♣3 and the ♠A on the ♠2. The ♥5 is packed on the ♥6, the ♣Q with the ♣J

on the ♣K and the ♦3 on the ♦4. The ♠2 with the ♠A is packed on the ♦3, and the ♣3 with the ♣2 on the ♣4.

Napoleon's square

HOW TO PLAY

First, 48 cards are played face up to the board in 12 piles of four cards, arranged as three sides of a square (see illustration).

The object of the game is to play the eight Aces, as they become available, to the centre of the square as foundations, on which to build ascending suit sequences to the Kings.

The top cards of the piles are exposed. They may be built on the foundations, or packed on each other in descending suit sequences. All cards in sequence at the top of a pile may be lifted as a whole and played elsewhere, and the vacancy, when all the cards of a pile have been moved, may be filled by a card or sequence from the top of another pile, by a card from the stock or by the top card of the waste heap.

The stock is dealt one card at a time and any card that cannot be built on a foundation or packed on the layout is played to a waste heap, the top card of which is always available to be played. The stock may be dealt only once. The player is permitted to look at all of the cards in a pile.

With the layout shown, the ♥A is played to the centre, the ♠5 is packed on the ♠6 and the ♦3 on the ♦4. Either ♣Q may be packed on the ♣K and the cards in those piles should first be looked at to determine which would be best.

Paganini

Paganini is a double-pack patience game, similar in principle to the single-pack game known as Vacancies (see page 72). It was composed by Mr Charles Jewell.

HOW TO PLAY

The entire pack is dealt face up on the table in eight rows of 13 cards each (see illustration, overleaf).

The object of the game is to arrange the cards so that each row consists of one suit beginning with an Ace (on the left) and ending with a King (on the right). No row is singled out for any particular suit; the player should choose, but must stick to this decision.

Play begins by moving one of the Aces to the extreme left of a row. This means that as the game proceeds the whole of the layout is in effect moved one space to the left. When a card is moved it leaves a space in the layout which is filled with the next higher card of the same suit as the card to the left of the space. Filling that space leaves another space in the layout and this is filled in turn in the same way, and so on, until a run is brought to an end by removing a card from the right-hand side of a King, because no card can be played to the space on the right of a King.

The game calls for a show of skill. To begin, a player has to decide which of the eight Aces he will move first and to which of the eight rows he will move it. Then, whenever a card is moved in the layout, there is, at least early in the play, a choice of two cards to fill the available space. It will be seen, therefore, that when all eight Aces have been moved to the extreme left of the layout, each move will offer the choice of filling one of eight spaces with either of the two suitable cards.

The layout in the illustration is not as difficult as it may appear. Indeed, with a little care the game should be won.

After a general survey of the possibilities in the game, the ♥A in the bottom row should be moved to the extreme left of the row; the ♥Q in the fifth row is moved to the space left vacant by the ♥A; and the ♣9 in the bottom row is moved into the space left vacant by the ♥Q. The space left vacant by the ♣9 may be filled either with the ♥2 in the second row or the one in the seventh row. Consideration shows that it should be filled with the one in the second row, because the ♣6 in the top row can be moved into the vacant space. The ♣A in the fifth row can be moved to the extreme left of the top row, and the ♣2 in either the second or fourth row can be moved into the space (alongside the ♣A) left vacant by the ♣6. Play continues until the game is won or no more moves can be made because all the spaces are to the right of Kings.

Parallels

HOW TO PLAY

An Ace and a King of each suit are removed, the Aces arranged in a column to the left of the board and the Kings to the right. A row of ten cards is dealt face up between the two columns (see illustration).

The object of the game is to build ascending suit sequences to the Kings on the Aces, and descending suit sequences to the Aces on the Kings.

The cards in the row are available to be built on the foundations and the vacancies are filled from the stock. When play comes to a halt, a second row of ten cards is dealt below the first. The deal continues in this way until the stock is exhausted. The play is governed by the following rules:

Only cardsfrom the rows which have one of their shorter sides free are available to be built on the foundations

Cards must not be built on a foundation until all ten cards of a row have been dealt

When any vacancy is filled, all vacancies must be filled

A row of ten cards may not be dealt until all the vacancies have been filled

Vacancies must be filled from left to right and from top to bottom

There is no compulsion to build a card on a foundation

When the two top foundation cards of the same suit are in sequence, either may be reversed (see Glossary) onto the other, except the Ace or King foundations

Looking at the stock's top card before deciding on a play is not allowed

With the layout as shown, the ♥2 is built on the ♥A, the ♣Q on the ♣K, and the vacancies filled from the stock.

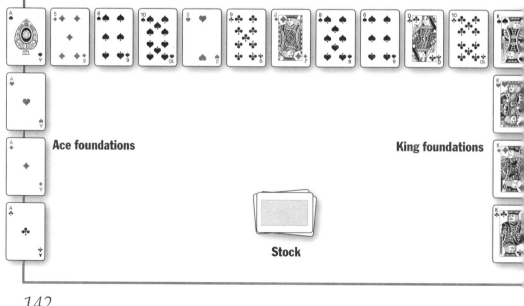

Ace foundations

King foundations

Stock

Parisian

Parisian is also called Parisienne, and is a variation on a game called Duchess de Luynes, or Grand Duchess.

HOW TO PLAY

An Ace and a King of each suit are played to the centre. Below them, four cards are dealt face up to the board, and two cards put aside face down (see illustration).

The object of the game is to build on the Aces ascending suit sequences to the Kings, and descending suit sequences to the Aces on the Kings.

The exposed cards in the layout are available to be built on the foundations. When no further play can be made, four cards are dealt from the stock to cover those cards in position and fill any vacancies, and two cards are put aside face down. Dealing is continued in this way until the stock is exhausted. When it is, the face-down cards are turned face up, and further plays, if any, are made with them and with the cards in the layout.

Four deals in all are allowed. To form a new stock, the piles in the layout are picked up and shuffled and the unplayed cards of the reserve are placed at the bottom of the pack. The redeals are made in the same way as the first deal, except that in the fourth, and final, deal all the cards are dealt face up to the layout, and no cards are put aside face down.

In the layout shown, the ♥2 is built on the ♥A and the ♦Q on the ♦K. As no more plays are to be made, four cards are dealt from the stock to fill the vacancies left by the ♥2 and ♦Q, and to cover the ♠6 and ♠4. Two more cards are dealt face down.

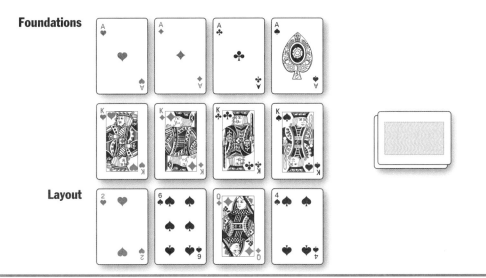

Foundations

Layout

Pendant

HOW TO PLAY

Pendant gets its name because the first 18 cards of the pack are arranged face up on the board in the form of a pendant: 12 cards are placed in pairs, close together, side by side, and then half-covered by six cards placed over them. A column of six cards is dealt face up on each side of the pendant, and the next card of the pack is played to the centre as the first foundation card (see illustration).

The object of the game is to release the other seven foundation cards, play them to the centre, and build on them round-the-corner suit sequences of 13 cards.

There is no packing on the layout. The cards in the outer columns and the bottom card, or cards, of the pendant are available to be built on the foundations. A vacancy in the pendant is not filled: a vacancy in a column must be filled, however, before any further play is made. If the top or bottom card of a column has been played, the vacancy may be filled with a card from either the stock or the bottom of the pendant; if any other card in a column has been played the vacancy must be filled from the stock.

The stock is dealt one card at a time, and any card that cannot be built on a foundation, or is not needed to fill a vacancy in a column, is played to a waste heap. When the stock is exhausted, the waste heap is picked up and redealt. Redealing continues until the game is either won or lost.

In the illustration, the foundation cards are established as the 8s, so the ♣8 and ♠8 are played to the foundation row. The ♥9 is built on the ♥8. Between each move the vacancies in the columns are filled. The vacancies left by the ♣8 and ♥9 must be filled from the stock; the vacancy left by the ♠8 may be filled either from the stock or by the ♦2. Obviously using the ♦2 is the better option because this will release the ♥10 and ♠J. The ♥10 is built on the ♥9, the ♥J on the ♥10 and the vacancy left by the ♥J filled by the ♠J. This releases the ♦8, which is played to the foundation row.

Foundation row

Pendant

Persian

Persian patience has the alternative name of Bezique patience, but the reason for this is not very clear. It could be because it is played with the 2s, 3s, 4s, 5s and 6s removed from the pack, as in bezique, but this also occurs in piquet and such a pack is more usually known as the short or piquet pack.

HOW TO PLAY

The 64 cards in the pack, after the low cards have been removed, are dealt, face up, to the board in eight overlapping rows of eight cards (see illustration).

The object of the game is to release the eight Aces, play them to the centre as foundations and build on them ascending suit sequences (the 7s follow directly on from the Aces) to the eight Kings.

The bottom cards of the columns are exposed. They may be built on the foundations, or packed on each other in descending sequences of alternating colours. A sequence may be moved only as a whole. A vacancy in the layout may be filled with any exposed card or sequence.

Three deals are allowed. After a deal the remaining cards in the layout are picked up and shuffled before being redealt in eight columns, which may now have fewer than eight cards in them. If no cards can be taken after the first deal it is not counted as one of the permitted three.

In the illustration, the ♦J is packed on the ♠Q and the ♥A played to the foundation row. The ♣8 is packed on the ♥9, the ♥7 on the ♣8, the ♠J on the ♦Q, the ♥8 on the ♠9 and the ♠A is played to the foundation row, and play continues in this way until the game is won.

Plait

HOW TO PLAY

First, 20 cards are dealt face up to the board, arranged in the form of a plait; that is, the first card is placed diagonally to the right, the second half covering it and diagonally to the left, the third half covering it and diagonally to the right, and so on to the twentieth card. A column of six cards is then dealt face up to the board on either side of the plait. The next card of the pack is dealt to the centre to determine the value of the foundation cards (see illustration).

As they become available the other seven cards of the same rank are played to the foundation row, to be built on in ascending, round-the-corner suit sequences of 13 cards each.

The bottom card of the plait and the exposed cards in the columns are available to be built on the foundations. The exposed cards in the columns are packed in descending suit sequences. A card played from the plait to a foundation or to a card in one of the columns is not replaced, but a card played from a column is. If the top or bottom card of a column is played, the player has the option of filling the vacancy with either the bottom card of the plait, the top card of the stock or the top card of the waste heap. If any other of the cards in the column are played the

vacancy must be filled with the top card of either the stock or the waste heap. Only one card may be moved at a time; cards must not be moved in sequences.

The stock is dealt one card at a time, and any card that cannot be built on a foundation or packed on the layout is played to the waste heap, the top card of which is always available for play.

When the stock is exhausted, the waste heap is picked up and redealt. Redealing continues until the game is either won or lost.

The game is a difficult one but interesting to play. Success depends very largely on making the best use of the cards in the plait.

In the illustration, the ♦9 is played to the foundation row and the vacancy is filled with the ♦8. The ♥9 is played to the foundation row, the ♥10 is built on the ♥9 and the ♥J on the ♥10. The vacancy left by the ♥J is filled with the ♦5, and the ♦9 is played to the foundation row. The vacancy left by the ♥10 is filled from the stock. The ♠6 is packed on the ♠7 and the vacancy filled from the stock.

Foundations

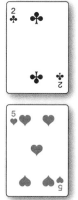

Plait

Reversi

Reversi is a simple building-up patience with the unusual feature that the foundation cards are built on in descending sequence, and the exposed cards in the layout packed in ascending sequence. The Ace is the lowest card of a suit.

HOW TO PLAY

The eight Kings are removed from the pack and arranged on the board in two rows of four cards. Ten cards are dealt face up to the board in two columns of five cards, one on either side of the foundation cards (see illustration).

The object of the game is to build descending suit sequences to the Aces on the Kings.

The cards in the layout are packed in ascending suit sequences and, providing the sequential order is retained, part or whole sequences may be moved from

one exposed card to another. A vacancy must be filled with a card from either the stock or the top of the waste heap. It must not be filled by any other card.

The stock is dealt one card at a time, and any card that is not played to a foundation or to the layout is played to the single waste heap, the top card of which is available for play. There is no second deal.

From the layout in the illustration, the ♥9 is packed on the ♥8, and the ♦5 on the ♦4. The ♣Q is built on the ♣K and the vacancies filled.

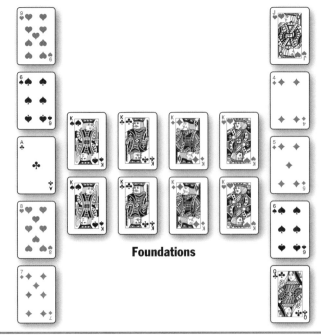

Foundations

Robin Post

Robin Post was composed by Colonel G.H. Latham, RE and it is one that calls for considerable thought and skill, not only because so many moves are available but because every move opens the door to a number of variations.

HOW TO PLAY

Two packs are shuffled together and 52 cards are dealt face up in rows of four, five, six, seven, eight, seven, six, five, four, with a space of one card's width between each card so that the cards only touch each other corner to corner, as in the illustration overleaf.

The object of the game is to release one Ace and one King of each suit, play them to the centre as foundations, and build ascending suit sequences to the Kings on the Aces, and descending suit sequences to the Aces on the Kings. At any stage of the play, if the top cards of two foundation piles of the same suit are in sequence, any or all of the cards of one pile (with the exception of the original Ace foundation or King foundation card) may be reversed onto the other (see Glossary).

The cards in the layout are subject to the following four rules:

A card that has two or more free corners may be lifted and played. In the illustration, the cards with two or more corners free are the ♠6 and ♦2 on the extreme edges of the layout, and those in the top and bottom rows. A card that has only one corner free may not be lifted and played, but other cards may be packed on it in either ascending or descending sequences of alternating colours. A card that has no corner free may neither be lifted and played nor packed on.
A moveable sequence must be moved as a whole, not in part, and may be reversed only onto a single card.

The remaining 52 cards of the stock are turned one at a time and played to the waste heap if they cannot be built on the foundation cards or packed on the cards in the layout. At any stage of the game, however, the layout may be refilled with cards from the stock. The cards must first be dealt to the original top row of the layout, from left to right, and, provided there are enough cards left in the stock, the layout must then be filled before any further moves are made either to the foundations or within the layout.

In the illustration (see following pages), the ♣Q in the top row can be packed on the ♦J at the left of the fourth row. Similarly the ♦10 in the top row can be packed on the ♠9 at the left of the second row. This will provide both the ♣A and ♠5 with two free corners and the ♣A may then be played to the centre as a foundation.

Royal cotillion

HOW TO PLAY

Arrange one Ace and one 2 of each suit in two columns, the 2s to the right of the Aces with a column-width between them. To the left of the Aces deal 12 cards in three rows of four cards – the left wing; and to the right of the 2s four rows of four cards – the right wing (see illustration).

The object of the game is to build suit sequences on the Aces in the order A, 3, 5, 7, 9, J, K, 2, 4, 6, 8, 10, Q and on the 2s in the order 2, 4, 6, 8, 10, Q, 3, 5, 7, 9, J, K.

Only the bottom cards of the columns in the left wing may be built on a foundation and the spaces are not filled, but any card from the right wing may be built on a foundation and the resulting

Left wing

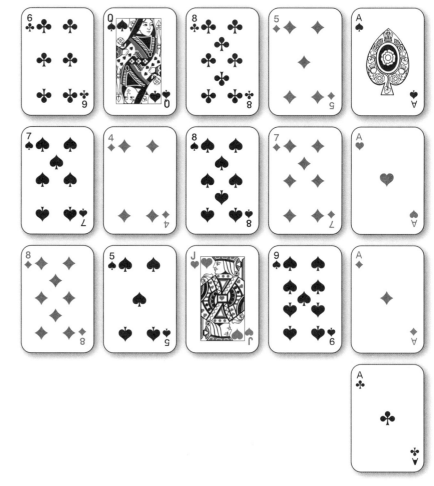

space must be filled with the top card of either the waste heap or the stock.

The stock is turned once and any card that cannot be built on a foundation, or is not needed to fill a space in the right wing, is played to the waste heap.

In the illustration, the ♥3 and ♠3 can be built on their respective Aces. This allows the ♠5 from the left wing to be built, allowing the ♦4 to be built on the ♦2. This allows ♦6 to be built, followed by ♦8 from the left wing releasing ♠7. Now ♦10 may be built on the ♦8.

Gaps in the right wing are now filled with cards from the stock and play continues.

Right wing

Royal parade

Royal Parade is a popular patience with the alternative names of Financier, Hussars and Three Up.

HOW TO PLAY

First, 24 cards are dealt in three rows of eight cards (see illustration). Aces take no part in the game and are discarded. The aim is to rearrange the cards in the layout so that the top row consists of eight 2s, the middle row of eight 3s, and the bottom row of eight 4s, and then build on these suit sequences at intervals of three cards, namely:

2 – 5, 8, J
3 – 6, 9, Q
4 – 7, 10, K

In the layout illustrated, the ♦ A, in the top row, and the ♣ A, in the bottom row, are discarded; the ♠ 4, in the middle row,

is moved to the space in the bottom row left vacant by the discard of the ♣ A, and the ♠ 7, in the top row, built on it. Either the ♥ 3 or ♣ 3, both in the top row, may be moved to fill the space in the middle row left vacant by the ♠ 4, and clearly the ♥ 3 should be chosen because the ♥ 6 in the bottom row may be built on it.

When all moves have been made, eight cards are dealt to waste heaps below the layout. Aces, as they are dealt, are discarded; other cards are used to build on the foundations or to fill spaces in the layout. Only the top cards of the waste heaps may be moved to the layout. Play continues in this way, with moves made after each deal of eight cards to the waste heaps, until the pack is exhausted.

Royal rendezvous

HOW TO PLAY

The eight Aces and a 2 of each suit are removed from the pack. The Aces are played to the centre in two rows of four, and two 2s on either side of the Aces. Below them, 16 cards are dealt face up to the board, and these may be arranged in any convenient way (see illustration).

The object of the game is to build ascending suit sequences to the Kings on the Aces in the upper row, ascending suit sequences to the Kings in the order A, 3, 5, 7, 9, J, K on the Aces in the lower row and ascending suit sequences to the Queens in the order 2, 4, 6, 8, 10, Q on the 2s.

All of the cards in the layout are available to be built on the foundation cards, and vacancies are filled from either the waste heap or from the stock if there is no waste heap.

The stock is dealt one card at a time and any card that cannot be built on a foundation is played to the waste heap, the top card of which is always available to be built on a foundation. The game ends when the stock is exhausted.

With the deal illustrated, the ♦3 is built on the ♦A in the lower row, the ♠4 on the ♠2, the ♣4 on the ♣2, the ♣6 on the ♣4 and the ♠2 on the ♠A in the upper row.

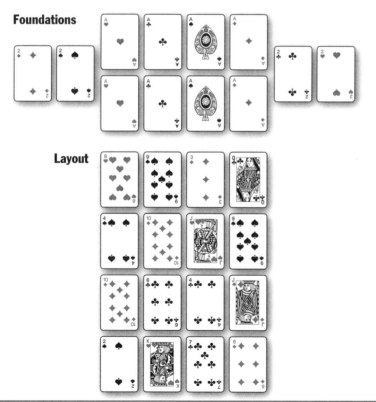

Foundations

Layout

Saint George

HOW TO PLAY

First, 48 cards are dealt face up to the board in four squares of 12 cards (four cards wide and three high) and the four squares arranged as a larger square with one card's width between them, forming a central cross (see illustration 1, top).

Counting the Kings as 13, the Queens as 12, the Jacks as 11 and the other cards according to the pips, the object of the game is to discard the whole pack by removing from the layout any two cards that together total 14 and that touch each other at the sides, the corners or top and bottom.

When a pair of cards has been discarded from the board, the vacancies are filled by closing up the remaining cards in the row or column towards a vertical or horizontal arm of the cross, whichever the player prefers. When all discards have been made, and the rows and columns closed up, the layout is filled with cards from the stock (see illustration 2, bottom). Although pairs can be made up from the different squares, cards may not be moved from one square to another during closing up. It is not compulsory to discard a pair of touching cards that total 14.

At the start of the game as dealt in illustration 1, the ♥J is paired and discarded with the ♦3 and both vacancies are immediately closed up.

The vacancy left by the ♦3 may be filled either with the ♠5 or the ♣2; it should be filled by the ♣2, which is paired and discarded with the ♠Q. The vacancy left by the ♥J is filled by the ♦9, which is paired and discarded with the ♠5. The vacancy left by the ♠Q is filled by the ♠K. The ♦K is paired and discarded with the ♠A and the vacancy left by the ♠A is filled by the ♥4. The ♦6 is paired and discarded with the ♠8.

Illustration 2 represents the situation when all possible cards have been paired and discarded, and the rows and columns closed up. The vacancies are now filled from the stock.

TACTICS

The game calls for foresight and it is also important to note that moving the cards in the angles of the cross is vital if the game is not to stagnate. Judicious pairing and discarding, coupled with skilful movement of the cards towards the arms of the cross, are needed to get the right card in position to pair with a card from the angle of the cross where it is holding up the game. Sometimes it is advisable not to discard a touching pair, and better to hold it in reserve so that it can be used for a more crucial play. The endgame usually contains a number of traps into which it is easy to fall. Exact play is necessary to win the game.

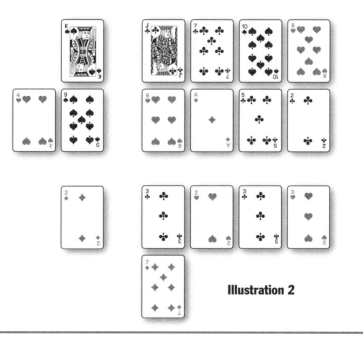

Illustration 1

Illustration 2

Saint Helena

Saint Helena, or Napoleon's Favourite, is a two-pack patience in which the packs are not shuffled together but used one after the other. Although the game gives the player some scope for ingenuity and remembering where cards are, it is such a simple game that one rather doubts that it really received its name through being Napoleon's chief amusement during his last years.

HOW TO PLAY

An Ace and a King of each suit are arranged in two rows, with the Kings above the Aces. A further 12 cards are dealt, clockwise, beginning above the left-hand King, as shown in the illustration.

The Kings are built on in descending suit sequences to the Aces, and the Aces in ascending suit sequences to the Kings with the following restrictions:

Cards dealt to spaces 1, 2, 3, 4 may be built only on the Kings

Cards dealt to spaces 7, 8, 9, 10 only to the Aces

Cards dealt to spaces 5, 6, 11, 12 to either Aces or Kings

When all possible moves have been made the spaces are filled from the pack and then, when no further moves can be made, another 12 cards are dealt to cover the cards in position.

When the pack has been exhausted, the restrictions are lifted, and cards may be built on any foundation from any one of the 12 surrounding waste heaps. In addition, the top card of each waste heap may now be packed on any other waste heap either in ascending or descending suit sequence, which helps to free the cards underneath.

Three deals in all are allowed. The waste heaps are picked up in reverse order: 12, 11 and so on down to 1, and turned face down, so that the bottom card of the twelfth waste heap becomes the top card of the remade stock. No shuffling is allowed.

Salic law

HOW TO PLAY

The eight Queens are discarded and play no part in the game.

One King (it does not matter which) is removed from the pack and played to the left of the board. Then a column of overlapping cards are dealt on it, face up, until another King is turned up. This second King is placed to the right of the first and more cards dealt on it until a third King is found. The deal continues in this way until there are eight columns of cards, which may be of irregular length, each headed by a King.

The Aces are played to a foundation row immediately above the Kings as soon as they appear. The object of the game is to build on the Aces sequences regardless of suit and colour up to the Jacks. The bottom card of a column is always available to be built on a foundation, and may be built on one while the deal in progress (see illustration).

Once all the cards have been dealt, the play continues. The bottom cards of the columns are available to be played on the foundations and, in addition, when, and only when, all of the cards have been dealt from the stock, a bare King (all the cards dealt on it having been played to the foundations) is equivalent to a vacancy, and any available card may be used to fill it.

The game is not as difficult as it may appear from the description, and the player should win one out of every three or four games. During the deal it is important to build on the foundations in such a way that there will be at least one vacancy on which to begin manoeuvring when the deal has been completed. Except for this, however, the foundations should not be built too high during the deal.

The game has been given the name of Salic Law after the code which unjustly excluded women from succession to the throne in certain European countries, like France and Spain. However, some players place the discarded Queens in a row above the Aces, so that while taking no part they look down in superior fashion to the action below, and if the game succeeds appear in a row above the Jacks and Kings.

The play on the deal in the illustration is as follows. The Ace foundations were built up during the deal to the levels shown. The ♥7 is built on the ♥6 and the ♣7 on the ♦6. The ♦8 is built on the ♥7 and the ♣9 followed by the ♣10 from above it on the ♦8. The ♠6 is built on the ♣5 and the ♠7 on the ♠6. The ♦9 is packed on the ♥K, the ♣8 is built on the ♠7 and the ♦9 on the ♣8. And so on.

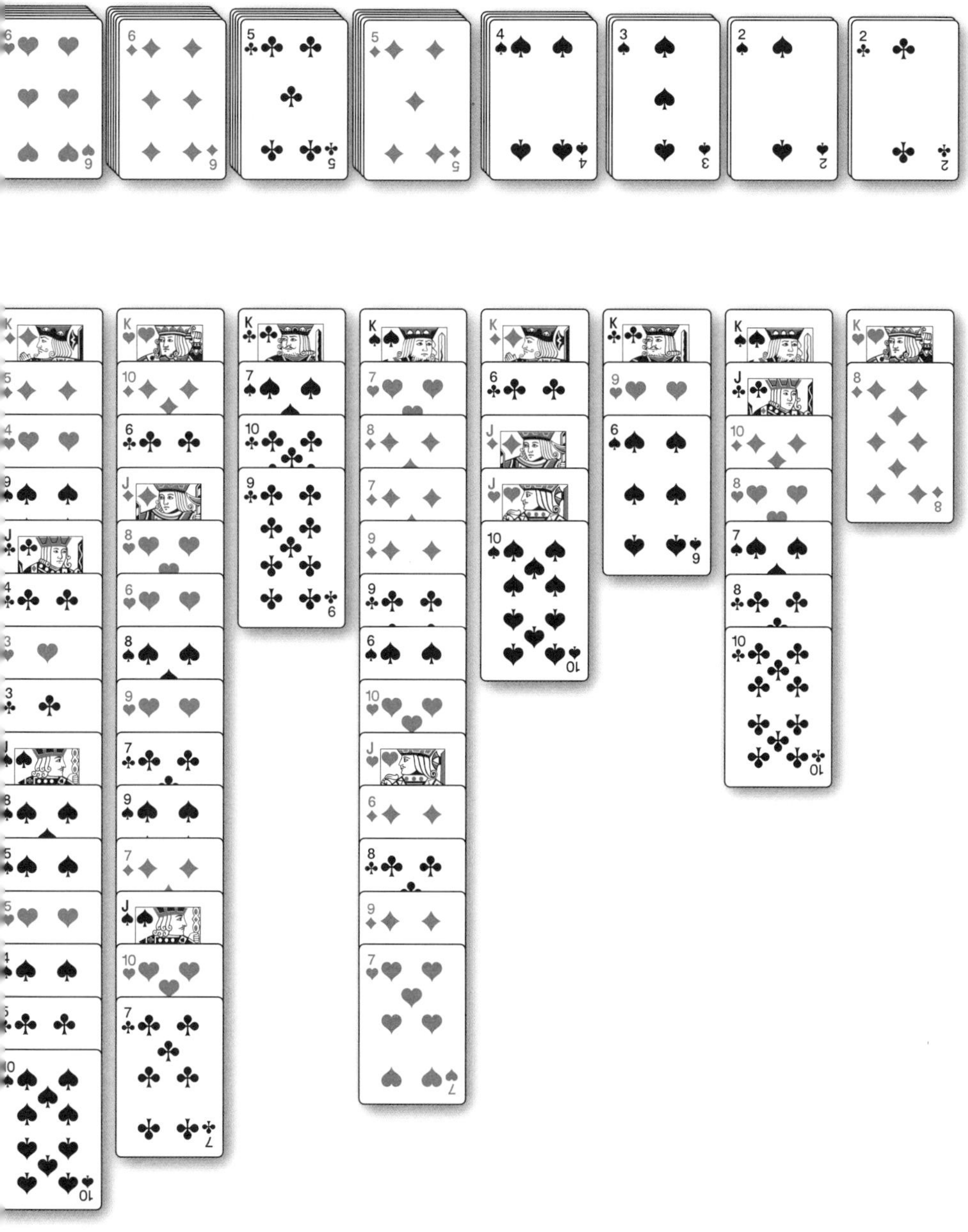

Shah

The Shah, or Star, derives both its names from its layout.

HOW TO PLAY

The ♥K is placed in the centre of the table, the other seven Kings are discarded (they take no part in the game) and the eight Aces are arranged about the ♥K, as illustrated.

The object of the game is to build suit sequences to the Queens on the Aces, so, if the game succeeds, the ♥K (the Shah) will be surrounded by the eight Queens.

A card is dealt to the outside of each Ace. If a 2 is dealt it is played to its foundation and another card is dealt to fill the vacancy. In the same way, if a 2 has already been played to a foundation and a 3 is dealt it is played to the foundation.

Three deals are made to the outside of the Aces and after this the outside cards are packed in descending suit sequences. Suit sequences can be packed as a whole from one outside card to another. Only the outermost card in a ray may be moved.

In the layout , the ♦4 may be packed on the ♦5, the ♥8 on the ♥9, the ♣4 on the ♣5, the ♠8 on the ♠9, and so on.

The stock is turned one card at a time, and those cards that cannot be built on a foundation or packed on the layout are played to a waste heap, the top card of which is always available to build or pack.

If all the cards in one ray are played, the space may be filled by one card from elsewhere in the outer circle.

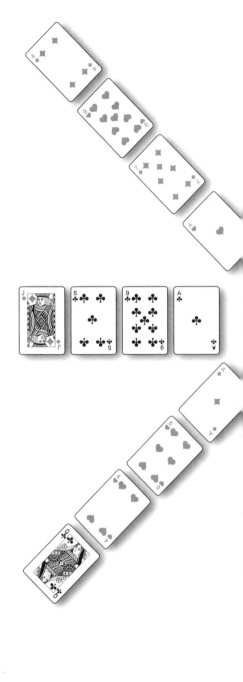

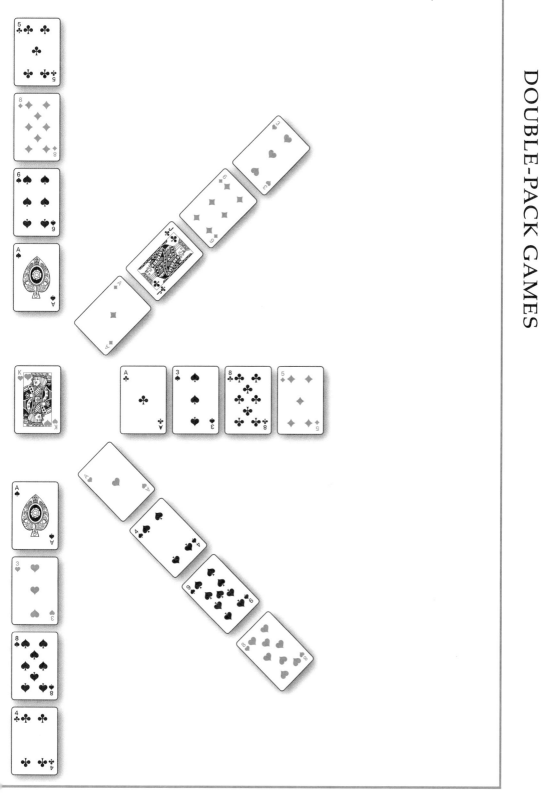

Sly fox

HOW TO PLAY

An Ace and a King of each suit are removed from the pack and the Aces played in a column to the left of the board, and the Kings in a column to the right of the board, to serve as foundations. Between the columns 20 cards are dealt face up in four rows of five cards each (see illustration).

The object of the game is to build ascending suit sequences to the Kings on the Aces, and descending suit sequences to the Aces on the Kings.

The cards are not packed in the layout, but they are all available to be built on the foundations, and any vacancy created in this way is immediately filled by a card from the stock. When all possible moves have been made and the vacancies filled, cards are dealt one at a time from the stock, and any card that cannot be built on a foundation is played to cover any card in the layout that the player wishes. When, and only when, all the cards in the layout have been covered, cards may be played from the layout to the

Ace foundations

foundations. The play is continued in this way until the stock is exhausted, and the game brought to an end.

Beginning with the position illustrated and with the vacancies created being filled immediately, the ♣Q is built on the ♣K, the ♦Q is built on the ♦K and the ♦J on the ♦Q. The ♥2 is built on the ♥A and the ♠2 on the ♠A.

TACTICS

The skill in playing this game lies in the choice of how to play the cards from the stock to cover the cards in the layout in such a way that cards that will shortly be needed are not blocked by cards that will not be required until later on. One card in the layout should be reserved for Aces and Kings and another for Queens and Jacks. Care should be taken to avoid a self-block by packing duplicate cards in opposite directions, and not in the same direction. It is a far from difficult game, and rarely fails to come out unless the player has made a mistake.

King foundations

Spider

There are several variations of Spider. The one described here is deservedly considered the best, and, indeed, among the best of all patiences, because it frequently calls for deep analysis. According to Redbook Magazine it was the favourite patience of President Franklin D. Roosevelt.

HOW TO PLAY

First, 40 cards are dealt to the table in four overlapping rows of ten cards each: the first, second and third rows face down, the fourth row face up, as in the illustration.

Foundation cards are not played to the centre: the aim of the game is to build within the layout descending suit sequences to the Aces on the eight Kings. Completed sequences are discarded, so the game is won when the table is cleared of all cards.

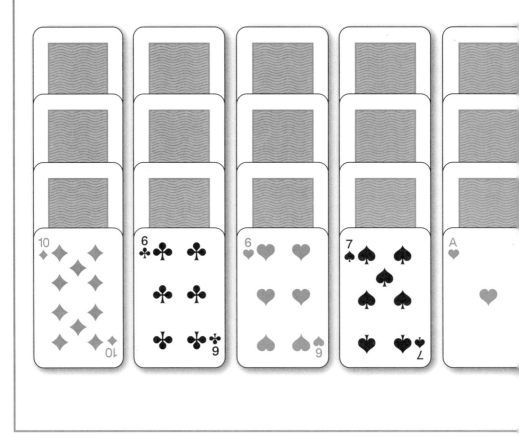

The cards at the bottom of the columns may be packed in descending sequences irrespective of suit and colour, and when a card is moved from one column to another the face-down card immediately above it is turned face up and becomes available for play.

In the diagram, any of the three 6s may be packed on the ♠7 and the ♦9 may be packed on either of the 10s. Two cards will thus be exposed.

When all of the cards have been moved from a column, the space may be filled by any exposed card or sequence.

After all possible moves have been made, and all the available spaces filled, ten more cards are dealt from the stock, face up, one to the bottom of each column, overlapping the cards there.

Play is continued in this way until the stock is exhausted. The last deal from the stock will be of only four cards.

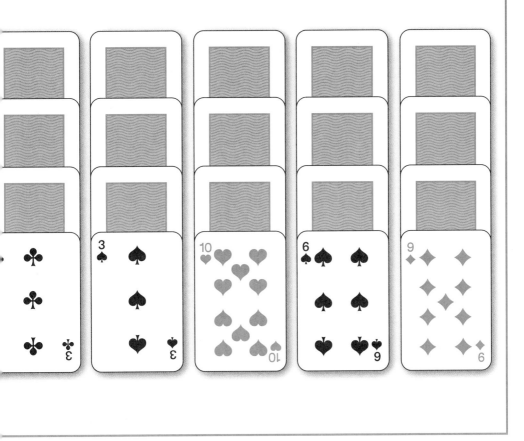

Sultan

Sultan, sometimes, but rarely, known as Emperor of Germany, is a two-pack patience that calls for some skill if it is to be successful.

HOW TO PLAY

The eight Kings and one ♥A are taken from the pack and arranged on the table as shown in the illustration. With the exception of the central ♥K, they serve as foundations to be built up in suit sequences to the Queens, with the Aces ranking between the Kings and the 2s.

A column of four cards is dealt face up to either side of the foundations, as shown in the illustration. This is known as the divan, and the cards dealt to it are available for building on the foundations. When one is played, the space is filled either from the stock or from the waste heap, but need not be filled immediately.

The stock is turned one card at a time to a waste heap, and may be dealt three times. In the illustration, none of the cards in the divan is playable to a foundation, so the game begins with the first card being turned from the stock.

TACTICS

Management of the divan is of great importance. Do not fill a space with a card unlikely to be wanted during the deal. If, for example, a foundation is built up to a 7, and both 8s are already buried, the 9s and higher cards should be played to the waste heap, because if used to fill a space in the divan they would be wasted.

Switchback

HOW TO PLAY

The eight Kings should be discarded because they are not needed.

One Ace of each suit is removed and these are placed in a square in the centre of the board, to serve as foundations, then 12 cards are dealt in a circle around them (see illustration).

The object of the game is to build suit sequences on the Aces in the order: A, 2, 3, 4, 5, 6, Q, J, 10, 9, 8, 7 and then, in reverse, 7, 8, 9, 10, J, Q, 6, 5, 4, 3, 2, A.

The cards in the circle may be built on the foundations and the vacancies filled from the stock or one of the waste heaps.

The stock is dealt one card at a time, and any card that cannot be built on a foundation is played to whichever waste heap the player chooses.

The stock is dealt only once, but the player has the grace (see Glossary) of shuffling each waste heap once.

Success depends very largely on how the player distributes the cards among the waste heaps. It is, however, not such a difficult game as it may seem, because at every turn of a card there are 17 cards to choose from – 12 in the circle, the four top cards of the waste heaps and the top card of the stock.

With the deal as illustrated, the ♠2 is built on the ♠A and the ♠3 on the ♠2. The vacancies are filled from the stock, because, as yet, there are no waste heaps.

Foundations

Terrace

Also known as Signora and Queen of Italy, this is an excellent patience which calls for considerable foresight. Its special feature is that all the blocking cards (the problems you will have to dodge round) are laid out in a line at the beginning.

HOW TO PLAY

Two packs are shuffled together and 11 cards dealt out in an overlapping line – the 'terrace' – so that they can all be seen. Space should be left below them for the eight foundations which will be built on. Below that, four cards are dealt out side by side and careful consideration is now needed because one of them must be chosen as the first foundation and played to the building area. The other seven cards of the same rank should be played there as they appear. The choice of foundation will depend on the cards in the terrace.

The gap left empty by removing the foundation card should be filled from the stock, and another five cards added to make a row of nine. These form the working area, where packing is allowed. Packing is continued, the foundation cards played to the building area as they appear and the gaps filled from the stock as necessary. When no more moves can be made and there are no gaps to fill, the cards in the stock can be turned over one by one to form a waste pile, the top card of which is available for packing. Once the end of the pack is reached, there is no redeal – if the cards are not all built onto the bases by then the game is over.

Cards are built up on the foundations in increasing sequences, alternating between red and black cards and turning the corner from King to Ace to 2 when you reach it. The exposed cards in the working area, the top card of the waste pile and the top card of the terrace are available for building.

Within the working area, packing is done in descending sequence, alternating red and black cards, turning the corner from 2 to Ace to King as necessary. Only one card at a time may be moved – sequences in the working area can only be moved by building – and gaps that appear may only be filled with the top card of the waste pile. Cards from the terrace may not be used for packing – they must be built directly. The only cards available for packing are single cards in the working area and the top card of the waste pile.

The illustration shows a game shortly after the waste pile has been started. Kings were chosen as the foundation cards, and three of them have been found. One of these has been built up to a black 3, getting rid of the first two cards of the terrace in the process. In order to get rid of the next card, the ♣9, it will be necessary to find a red 4, a black 5, and so on up to a red 8 (the 5, the 6 and the 8 are already waiting in the working area, so this won't be too difficult). Note that it is illegal to pack the ♥8 and ♠9 onto the ♥10 in the working area, since only one card may be moved at a time.

TACTICS

The art of getting this game of patience to turn out is to work out in advance where the terrace cards are going to go, and not to do any building that does not contribute directly to this aim. For much of the time you will be turning cards from the pack to the waste pile, waiting for some particular card to come up so that you can remove the top card of the terrace. While doing this, though, you can prepare a 'reception committee' for the next cards in line down the terrace. It hardly matters how big the waste pile becomes – you will find that it has an almost magical way of disappearing once the terrace has been lost. With care this patience can be turned out successfully about half of the time.

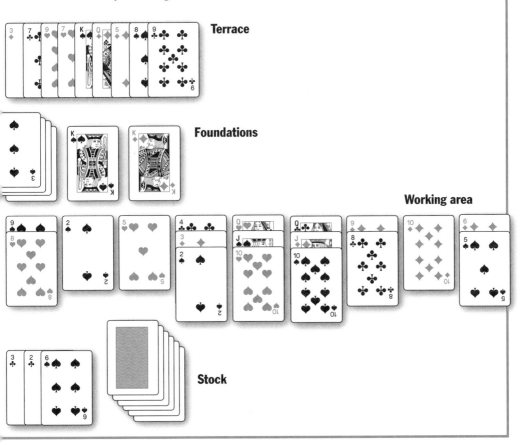

Terrace

Foundations

Working area

Stock

Windmill

The game known as Windmill or Propeller gets its name from the layout.

HOW TO PLAY

Any King is placed face up on the table, and two cards are dealt above it, two below it, and two on either side of it, to form a cross (see illustration). The first four Aces that are dealt, whether to the layout or as the stock is turned, are played to the inner angles of the cross.

The object of the game is to build on the central King a descending, round-the-corner sequence of 52 cards (i.e. four complete sequences of King to Ace following one another), regardless of suit and colour, and ascending suit sequences, regardless of suit and colour, to the Kings on the four Aces.

In the layout shown, the ♦ A is played to an angle of the cross, the ♦ Q is built on the ♠ K, and the ♥ J on the ♦ Q. At any time a card may be taken from an Ace foundation and played to the King foundation, but only one card may be taken from each Ace foundation during the building of any one of the four sequences based on the King foundation.

The stock is turned to a waste heap, and vacancies in the layout must be filled from the waste heap, or from the stock if there is no waste heap.

There is no second deal, but when the stock is exhausted, the waste heap may be taken up and the first card dealt. If it can be played to a foundation, the next card is dealt, and so on. The game, however, comes to an end when no card can be played to a foundation.

Glossary

Available card – A card that may be played as the rules of the game permit.

Blocked – A card so situated that it cannot be moved without infringing the rules of the game.

Board – The flat surface on which the game is played

Build – To place a card on a foundation-card in such order as the rules of the game dictate.

Centre – The unoccupied part of the board above the layout.

Column – Two or more cards placed perpendicularly on the board, one immediately below the other, or slightly overlapping each other for convenience.

Court cards – the Jack, Queen, King of each suit (also known as picture cards)

Exposed card – A card at the bottom of a column, extreme right of a fan, or the top of a foundation-pile or waste-heap, which may be played on, or moved, subject to the rules of the game. Also, a face-down card is said to be exposed when it is turned face up.

Fan – Two or more cards arranged on the board in open formation, like a fan.

Foundation card – A card played to the centre, and on which a complete suit or sequence has to be built in accordance with the rules of the game.

Foundation pile – The cards built on the foundation-card in accordance with the rules of the game.

Foundation row – The foundation-cards arranged in a row in the centre.

Grace – The privilege limited to some games of making an illegal move.

Heel – A number of cards counted out at the beginning of the game and placed apart to be used as directed by the rules of the game.

Layout – The cards laid out on the board in a prescribed pattern to be moved or packed on in accordance with the rules of the game.

Numeral cards – Ace to 10 of each suit

Pack – To place a card on one exposed in the layout in such order as the rules of the game dictate.

Picture cards – see Court Cards

Reversing – in two-pack patiences in which cards are simultaneously built in ascending order on Ace foundations, and descending order on King foundations, when the top cards are in sequence (i.e. the Ace foundation is built up to a 7 and the King foundation down to the 8) it is sometimes allowed for cards to be built as required from one to the other, or reversed from one foundation to the other (see Corner Stones, page 92).

Row – Two or more cards placed horizontally on the board, side by side, or slightly overlapping each other for convenience.

Sequence – Two or more cards following one another in correct order, but not necessarily of the same suit.

Sequence, Ascending – A sequence progressing from low to high (e.g. Ace to King).

Sequence, Descending – A sequence progressing from high to low (e.g. King to Ace).

Sequence, Round-the-corner – A sequence in which the highest card is considered adjacent to the lowest (e.g. 3, 2, A, K, Q or Q, K, A, 2, 3).

Sequence, Suit – A sequence in which all the cards are of the same suit.

Stock – The undealt cards of the pack which may be used later in the game.

Vacancy – An unoccupied space in the layout.

Waive – The privilege limited to some games of lifting a card in order to play the one underneath it.

Waste heap – The pile of cards consisting of those that could not be played either to a foundation pile or to an exposed card in the layout.

Worrying back – The privilege limited to some games of returning cards from the foundation piles to the layout.

Index

ACKNOWLEDGEMENTS

Executive Editor Trevor Davies
Editor Sharon Ashman
Design Manager Tokiko Morishima
Design and Illustrations Publish on Demand Ltd
Production Controller Jo Sim